Lee Primeau

Mission_Shift

**Great Commission Living
in a Postmodern World**

Strategies for Developing
Cross-Cultural
Communication Skills

Mission_Shift
Author
Lee Primeau

Published by
The Master's Foundation
1290 Eglinton Ave. Suite 5
Mississauga, ON L4W 1K8

Cover Design by:
Gary Hendrick
BlessAd Advertising
gary@hendrick.ca

ISBN - 1-895918-11-1

Printed in Canada

Copyright © 2003 by Lee Primeau
        Leader_Shift

All rights reserved. This publication may not be reproduced, in a retrieval system, or transmitted in whole or in part, in any form or by any means electronic, mechanical, photocopying, recording or other wise, without prior written permission of the Publisher.

Dedication

This book is dedicated to:

*My mother, Mary Primeau
who expresses a life lived for others.*

*My father, Claude Primeau,
who mentored servanthood before the book was written.*

*My wife, Cathy Primeau
who expresses the consummate Proverbs 31 woman.*

*My sons, Jordan and Christopher,
who express the authenticity of their generation.*

Contents

Acknowledgements 7
Introduction 9

Chapter One
    Motives of Missions
    Dealing with Inner Issues 13

Chapter Two
    A Biblical Foundation for a World View 35

Chapter Three
    Why Bother? A Divine Set Up 61

Chapter Four
    Components of Cross-Cultural Communication . . . 81

Chapter Five
    Developing Cross-Cultural
    Communication Skills 99

Chapter Six
    The Eleven Mindsets Required
    for Cross-Cultural Communication 113

Chapter Seven
    The Global Reality and the Global Opportunity . . . 135

Chapter Eight
    Humility or Achievement? 149

Conclusion
    Why Short Term Missions? 171

Acknowledgements

This book is an attempt to distill, from a personal perspective, the last ten years of training and teaching in cross-cultural communications for short-term mission teams. Although I have often been the trainer or teacher, I have always been, first of all, a learner. The sources of that learning include a host of material and the contributions of others who have invested many years of experience in cross-cultural communication as well as in research.

The bulk of my learning has come from colleagues and students who have learned and tested the theories of cross-cultural communication. On the colleague side are: Steve Fry, Founder of the Messenger Fellowship, who constantly encouraged me and prodded me to finally get something down on paper; Keith Parks, founder of Seeds International, who created the opportunity for me to put my big toe into the water of publishing; Jim Craig, friend and editor superb who exercised grace and patience in helping me "get it"; Tom Morris, who dared to dream with me about this possibility; George Atkinson, one of the most significant mentors on the planet, who taught me principle and focus which made accomplishing this project possible; Les Hewitt, author of The Power of Focus and Founder of The Achievers Coaching Program, who imparted the success principles needed to realize the goal of publishing; and the Master's College and Seminary, Northwest Bible College and Calgary Leadership Training Center students who participated in my classes and provided insightful feedback. I also want to acknowledge "The Gang" who make up the team to bring Mission_Shift to publication — Gary Hendrick of BlessAd Advertizing, Stan Watrich of The Master's Foundation, and Paul Knowles of English Garden Publishers.

On a more informal basis, I must thank my wife Cathy for the encouragement and insight concerning such matters that Mission_Shift deals with, and Jordan and Christopher my sons, who invested much counsel in the content and provided an understanding of the generation this book is intended to serve, my inlaws Oscar and Eleanor Simpson for the countless hours of support, listening and advise.

Still further, I must acknowledge the Pentecostal Assemblies of Canada for providing an open door to participate in meetings and sit on committees that offered numerous lessons and insights reinforcing the principles of Mission_Shift. Of note are Randy Sonchen, Irving Whitt, Linda Duncalfe and Kory Sorensen of the World Missions Department (the service center!); in particular, the Implementation Team of the STMNetwork.ca — Pat Burling, Ian Stokes, Allan Waine, Owen Black, Eldon Wright, Brian Egert, Ron Rust, Rauni Salminen, Bob Dewling, Dave Slater, Darcy McAlister and Mark Running.

In the spirit of this acknowledgement, the operative word is "attempt." I am attempting to acknowledge those who have helped me, but in truth there are so many individuals and organizations upon whose shoulders I stand, it is impossible to list them all. However, their importance and significance is not internationally overlooked — I ask for understanding of the limitation of one's mind to comprehend the overwhelming contributions others make throughout a lifetime.

So this is just an attempt to say — Thank you! Thank you for the challenges, the insights, and the friendships.

Introduction

According to an article in a recent Christianity Today magazine, an estimated one million people from North America are mobilized in short term mission trips each year. These numbers are staggering; they utterly eclipse previous totals. This is powerful evidence of an emerging generation embracing the Great Commission at a pace never thought possible.

Missiologists have called short term missions the third wave of missionary activity since the event of the cross. In my experience with short term missions over the past twenty-five years, I have come to see, first hand, how individuals making themselves available to God can have an enormous impact for the Kingdom of God upon this world.

The local church is the only organization that exists for those outside itself. When this truth is compromised, focus is lost and purpose dissipates. However, when the local church engages in the Great Commission in a proactive and intentional way, there is a "releasing" in the supernatural realm. All manner of people, ministries, finances, and opportunities are unleashed into the mission to see others come to Christ.

This generation is fueled by the post-modern reality that creates an opportunity to be authentic, sacrificial, community-conscious, and effective. In many ways, this is an opportunity that the past generation did not experience. We live in a time of non-absolutes, in which people believe that reality is based upon what one defines as true, and in which Heaven is what one interprets it to be. But the emerging generation of believers has found true absolutes, it has taken hold of experience in Jesus and absoluteness in Jesus. This generation has discovered the planet's greatest power for change and source for meaning. Jesus really is the Answer!

The blending of belief without evidence and faith in faith itself may at first sound very dangerous; and it can be. But this also offers up a context with which to work, an opportunity that has not been taken advantage of by the church since the realization of Postmodernity.

At the same time, recent global events and the new realities of uncertainty have provided a clarion call for the church to pray about, be aware of, and now take action with regards

> This is powerful evidence of an emerging generation embracing the Great Commission at a pace never thought possible.

to, the immense need and opportunity to share Christ with others in the world. For this present generation, the slogan has become, "we change lives ... that's what we do".

There is a new awareness of the validity of differing educational systems, and of the realities that for the first time in the history of human civilization there is more information outside the classroom than inside it, and that the modus operandi of personal development, academically and spiritually, has shifted from the sage on the stage to the guide on the side. This is fueling the ability of the church to mobilize people much more quickly, enhance the quality of those mobilized, do it at a much lower cost, and with much more security.

This book is about developing a framework for successful and effective short term missions operations. Simply said, we want to send out people who are better equipped for the task at hand.

I have intentionally set the tone of the book by first dealing with the personal motives for missions, believing that unless the heart is right and pure there is a great risk that the activities engaged in make no sense, have no effect, and leave no lasting impact.

In chapter two the concept of world view is the theme. This is intended to enable the short term mission participant or team member to begin to see the world through a different lens, other than personal bias, human condition, cultural preference, or ignorance altogether. These concepts are not easy to grasp and more difficult to incorporate into one's own life. If they were easy, there would be no need to give so much attention to them. However, the lack of processing these principles has led to ineffectiveness, frustration, and the discrediting of short term missions — a negative result which is totally unnecessary.

Chapter three of Mission_Shift deals with developing a biblical foundation for short term missions. It is an attempt to answer why we do the things we do, and for whom do we do them. This chapter focuses on God as the primary reason we engage in missions, as well as developing out the Great Commission as read in the Gospel of Luke.

The two subsequent chapters begin to unpack the training aspect of cross cultural communication. They are based on the assumption that anyone desiring to follow the call of God upon their lives desires to be the best possible, for the glory of God and for the benefit of those to whom they are heading out to minister. These chapters deal with how to be a better communicator, a more aware cross cultural worker, and an excellent missionary.

It is not unusual for those who attend my seminars or enroll in my classes, who have had experience living in a foreign field, to express the need for this information or to ask where this information was when they really and truly needed it. If I write this book for anyone, it is for those people, and it is in response to the painful expressions on their faces asking for material like this to be made available for those going into the mission field. If there is a passion lying behind this work, it is to somehow communicate to those who have no idea how important it is to be properly prepared; to bring them to a point where they "get it". Chapter six addresses this, in attempting to create eleven mindsets that will create proper approaches to short term missions.

I wrote Chapter seven to attempt to put an exclamation point on the context and culture in which we are being called to minister. We live in both a reality and an opportunity, and we will be held accountable for what we have done to make a difference.

Chapter eight takes a look at the dynamic tension between the walk of humility and the need to press toward the goal to achieve. This chapter intentionally addresses leadership and is designed to apply to everyone who engages in misions hence exercising leadership.

The conclusion answers the question, "Why short term missions?" This is intended to clarify some overall questions about the mission to which we are called.

As you read and muse over the content of this book, I trust you will pick up a passion to serve, and to serve with excellence of spirit. If you are a leader, my hope is that this book will be a catalyst for you to continue to explore information and opportunities to further prepare your teams with a higher level of expertise, in order to make a significant difference. For those using this book in a team context, I pray that it will become a field manual, referred to regularly in order to call each team member to accountability.

In His Service,

Lee Primeau

CHAPTER ONE

Motives of Missions
Dealing with Inner Issues

I was in a church service several years back when a very interesting incident occurred. During the worship service, someone came in through the back entrance of the 2000-plus-seat sanctuary and ran to the front of this somewhat conservative congregation. All along the way, he was shouting loudly that he needed help in a desperate way; the shock of his entrance immobilized even the trained ushers who were supposed to be prepared for such things.

As the person stood gazing into the congregation, no one knew if they had a severely disturbed person in their midst; was this someone who might do something drastic and devastating? Without hesitation, the senior pastor moved out from the pulpit and went down to meet the person. Putting his arm around him, he assured the congregation that everything was okay, and that the person had come to the right place for help. As the pastor stood there, arm around the person, he began to lead in songs that seemed to bring peace to the person and to the congregation. It was not long before the tense situation was resolved, the person was taken care of in a loving way, and we all learned something about transparency and right motives.

I am sure you have found your self in tense situations such as this, and that you have had the opportunity to observe either your own or a leader's reaction. It is times like these when the spirit of a person truly comes out. And this is the subject of this first chapter of Mission_Shift. In order to properly and effectively communicate cross culturally, a shift must occur in our own hearts and minds that leads, in any environment, to an automatic response of love and compassion in place of withdrawal and indifference.

Primary motives:

Without the right motive, nothing gets done right. Nothing. That is fundamental. Motives are the core, the centre from which all things spring forth. As we begin this book, I cannot stress too strongly that motives make all the difference. This is the one driving value, the one foundational truth, no matter what language is spoken or which culture is entered into.

There's an old cliché: "if you only learn one thing from this book, let it be this" — without the right motive, nothing gets done right.

We are accustomed to hearing about people who have "mixed motives." Sadly, when it comes to our leaders in many fields, we almost expect this to be true. A key word that points to our suspicions in this area is the word "political". When we say someone is "political" or a company or organization is "political", what we are essentially saying is that there are mixed motives and hidden agendas that create suspicion or doubt. We are, in fact, bringing into question the sincerity of a person or an organization.

The word "sincerity" comes to us from the French, where the root meaning is "without decay". "Sincerity" is in turn used to translate a common Greek word from the New Testament which literally means "judged by sunlight."

Without the right motive, nothing gets done right. Nothing. That is fundamental. Motives are the core, the centre from which all things spring forth.

How does that translate into "sincerity," you ask? I think the story is fascinating: the words we understand as "sincere" and "sincerity" in biblical times referred to the true quality of an artisan's work in sculpture. Most of us are aware that sculpture was one of the premier art forms during the Greek and Roman eras — biblical times. Statues from that period are prized by museums around the world to this day.

Cities in New Testament times were filled with stone sculptures, and these artists were kept very busy. The truth was, though, their work was not always perfect. From time to time, when a sculptor was carving the stone for a statue, a chunk of stone would break off at the wrong place. But good sculpting stone was expensive, and the carvers would be reluctant to abandon a project because of one error. The solution? Wax would be made up of the same color as the stone, and was molded to fill the missing piece of the statue. The only problem was, when that statue was exposed to direct, hot sunlight, the wax would melt away, exposing the flaw of the statue. The solution to this was that all the true statues were designated to be placed in the center of the roads and markets where they could stand the heat with no flaws to be exposed. The statues that were fixed with the wax were placed at the sides where the shade would protect them from the heat, and the flaws could be kept secret.

An honest piece of sculpting would be "judged by sunlight" – "sincere."

In our Bibles, the terms "sincere" and "insincere" relate to this practice. So when we deal with motives for the things we do, especially in the work of the Kingdom, we are talking about motives that are either sincere — they can stand the heat of exposure — or insincere — mixed motives that do not honestly reflect the purity and the wholeness of the work of God. Flawed motives, once exposed, will show who we truly are.

Nowhere is this more evident than in the work of missions. The New Testament is full of references concerning operating with the right motives when engaged in the work of missions. Jesus was quick to criticize the Pharisees for their insincerity — they were concerned with doing good works in public in order to obtain public credit and praise, and not with doing good works quietly, without fanfare. Their "good works" were flaunted before their fellow men, not done quietly, in obscurity, before God alone. We also read the shocking and disconcerting story of Annias and Sapphira who were dealt a death blow by the Holy Spirit because they lied — a clear mark of false motives and insincerity.

As the early church began to form its identity, the requirements for leadership were specific and stern. Leaders were to take care of the people with love and patience and not to "lord it over them," creating hardship. That has never changed: the central focus in living the Christian life, in providing leadership, or in heading out into mission, must be to ensure proper motives are engaged.

> ...the central focus in living the Christian life, in providing leadership, or in heading out into mission, must be to ensure proper motives are engaged.

Now, let's be honest about sincerity: the reality is that, as human beings, our motives will always be an issue we need to bring before God on a constant basis. The Bible teaches us that our own hearts are sinful and deceitful above all else. We are poor judges of ourselves. We require the conviction of the Holy Spirit to correct us and keep us in line. We also need to be accountable to others who we trust and who we allow to "speak" into our lives. The book of Proverbs speaks of iron sharpening iron and that is what one person does to another. Confrontation and honest communication, in a safe environment, where we allow others to point out things in our lives that need closer examination, is a necessary and positive aspect of our Christian life.

Understanding God's love and compassion toward us in order to understand motives

In developing a "world view," the Christian must begin with answering two compelling and penetrating questions.

One is: Why do we do the things we do?

The second is: For whom do we do them?

These questions concentrate the mind and the spirit, focusing us on establishing the fundamental motivation for "being" a Christian and for "doing" Christian things such as living a holy life, sharing Christ with others, and taking the step of engaging in world missions.

All through the Bible (in both the Old Testament and the New Testament) we find that the underlying principle of why God does what He does is His unconditional and undying love for His creation. Now, the primary object of this book is neither to study God's motives nor to defend challenges concerning this point. To consider that specific topic in detail must be reserved for a discipline called apologetics. The good news is that, from New Testament times onward, scholars and writers have agreed the central point to the story of God and humanity is, "God so loved ...". So it is a safe and honest starting point for us.

Therefore, the point from which we all must launch ourselves, when engaging in Christian activity and sharing Christ, is the same one that launched a "sacred romance" in the heavenlies in eternity before time began. We start with a

> This sacred romance led to God calling out a person, a family, ultimately a nation in the Old Testament to reflect His character, His commitment, His protection, His forgiveness, His covenant character.

loving God who allowed man and woman to make a free choice — to serve Him, or not to serve Him and thus break off relationship through rebellion. It is the sacred romance of a God who loves His creation so much, He dared to be un-controlling and releasing. Perhaps the most frightening thing God created was this freedom. It is also one of the most beautiful things He created.

This sacred romance led to God calling out a person, a family, ultimately a nation in the Old Testament to reflect His character, His commitment, His protection, His forgiveness, His covenant character. It eventuated in God leading a people through the severest of conditions, the greatest of times, the lowest of circumstances and eventually to the zenith hour of eternity and history on the cross of Calvary where He ultimately revealed His compassion and love.

Biblical definitions of love:

Today, we have a problem with "love". No, I don't mean any of the things you are thinking at this moment, although they all may well be true. Here, I'm simply talking about the meaning of the word. We use "love" to describe everything from our feeling about fried food — "I love hamburgers" — to our reaction to cultural experiences — "I love Mozart" — to our relationship with another human being – "I love Amy" — to our connection with our creator — "I love God."

When a word means everything, it is in very great danger of meaning nothing. The Greeks had a better idea.

There was little chance of mistaking what a Greek meant when he or she used one of many words that we express with the four letters, "love". The Greeks were very specific in their vocabulary in this area. And that's the vocabulary of the New Testament, which was originally written in Greek.

One Greek word we often translate as "love" was "eros", a word you will recognize as the root of our word "erotic". Today this word conjures up all kinds of warped and twisted expressions of love in the sensual area. To the Greeks, it also meant a sensual love, but one that was intended to be healthy between two lovers as a natural expression of affection (however, as we learn from history, the result was not always healthy!).

A second term for "love" was "storge", which related to a love between family members and expressed the bond and commitment within that family.

A third term for love was "phileo", which suggests the camaraderie of a group of people with like interests. This could be a group of people involved in a union, sports team, or the like.

...the starting point for developing a world view as a believer is to understand the "Father Heart of God" as expressed in His love ("agape") and compassion for lost humanity.

Finally, there was a seldom-used word that expressed an unconditional love that neither required nor demanded anything in return. That word was "agape" — love on a much higher plane, so special that the word was strictly reserved for very specific usage. This is the term the Bible uses when it expresses God's love for His creation. For example: "God so agape-d (loved unconditionally, purely, absolutely, singularly) the world that He gave His only begotten son ..."

So the starting point for developing a world view as a believer is to understand the "Father Heart of God" as expressed in His love ("agape") and compassion for lost humanity. When we are captured by this truth, affected by this truth, and moved to action by this truth, then we are prepared to make a real difference in the world.

God Unlimited!

God's dominant attribute is depicted in Exodus 34:6-7, where He Himself characterizes His attitude toward humanity. Here God describes Himself as compassionate and gracious; slow to anger, and abounding in loyal love and faithfulness. He tells us He keeps loyal love for thousands, forgives sin and transgression and iniquity. He also says He doesn't let the guilty go unpunished and that there are generational consequences for not repenting.

Let's closely examine some of the words used in this passage from the Bible. First, the name God uses is "Lord," meaning "I Am That I Am". One serious mistake believers make when it comes to knowing and understanding God involves the limited definitions we apply to God. Depending on our background, family upbringing, the church we attend, or the education we have, there are experiences we have gained that "script" our definitions of certain things and certain people. Our understanding of God all too often depends on the "scripts" we have, arising from other relationships or experiences, which may be either negative or positive, but which none the less are not truly applicable to who God is, as revealed in biblical teaching. We color our perception of God by the scripts written by our experience with our parents, our teachers, or other authorities, and lay these scripts over our understanding of God, thus creating more of a caricature of Him than a clear picture of God.

We bring those experiences to our understanding of God. For example, when we call God "Father," it is hard not to understand the word "father" through our experience of our parents. Overall, we all reference God based on our experiences and, in the process, we limit our sense of who God is. We may understand Him as being permissive beyond correction, or punitive, or callous, or unforgiving, or demanding, or conditional.

Whatever our reference points, once we label God according to our scripts, we limit His significance in our lives and in the lives of those whom we are attempting to reach. We all have made decisions and commitments at one time or another based upon negative experiences that become limiting factors in our lives. For example, our counseling rooms are filled with jilted lovers who have vowed never to trust again because of past experiences with others. To import these experiences and vows into our image of God only creates an unstable spiritual relationship with Him that is distorted and lacks trust in Him.

Right from the beginning, God revealed Himself as the "I Am that I Am," meaning that He can and will be whatever we need Him to be in our particular circumstances. God reminds us that He cannot be put into a box (formed into our distortions based on negative experiences), He cannot be owned, He cannot be controlled! Imagine — He is a God who is always surprising us, always visiting us in a unique way, always bringing us hope, love, joy, peace and all good gifts in such amazing ways that we are always caught off guard. As we truly come to know this God, the true nature of our God will protect us from falling into the same old "scripts", the same old expectations. He is always so much more!

God the Gracious One:

The word gracious is literally intended to be understood as "having favor". The people repentant before God receive favor. In other words, grace means to grant favor — specifically, unmerited favor — to someone. God is gracious in all His dealings; but God's grace is most evident, most clear, in His desire to forgive sins and grant salvation to people.

And we, as God's people, are called to offer grace even as God has shown grace to us.

This can be a difficult, perhaps even terrifying concept for someone who has been raised to be unforgiving or bitter. One's ability to grant this kind of love to others may be hung up by a sense of injustice, or of the other being deserving of punishment, or by the desire for revenge itself. These "scripts", as we discussed above, can get in the way of our being messengers of the grace of God. They can also get in the way of our receiving God's gift, fully and freely.

This is just one example of a whole host of reasons that we can find ourselves misrepresenting the image of God to others. To understand that we are all sinners who deserve a sentence of death from God, but who instead have become the recipients of His unwarranted favor and forgiveness, is to begin to open the door to introduce others to the same experience.

> In trying to qualify for our salvation, we rob ourselves of the freedom that God in Christ brought us at the cross.

But, as noted briefly above, not only can it be a severe test for us humans to grant the grace of God unto others, it can also be a difficult challenge to understand and accept that we are recipients of that grace. For many reasons, it may be difficult to accept the grace of God. It's not uncommon for people to fall into trying to earn their salvation, to prove that we really deserve God's grace. What a foolish idea — all have sinned, all have fallen short, all can only know God's gracious salvation as a gift. We cannot live up to God's requirements; we can only accept His unmerited favor.

In trying to qualify for our salvation, we rob ourselves of the freedom that God in Christ brought us at the cross. We lose precious Kingdom time and become withholders of God's ultimate expression of Himself to others we meet. In such cases, as we try to carry the Good News to others, the terminology may be there, the activity may be there, the emotions may be there there, but the spirit of God's grace is inevitably absent, lost in our confusion over the need to earn the Kingdom, to be saved through earning salvation. Thus, we sabotage the whole mission.

The Good News — the "gospel" — is a message and a mission of grace, through Jesus. In order to be true carriers of the gospel message we must be living in the full realization of that grace ourselves.

God the Compassionate One:

The next term God uses to express who He is is the word "compassion". Compassion is a word related to the term "womb"; it suggests the state of being provided for in care and protection as one who is dependent and helpless. Here is where the "rub" is for us as believers, and at the same time the most powerful concept in the Bible. The Fall created in us a rebelliousness (literally, "sin") that moves us away from God and toward a motivation to "do things our own way". This is the root cause of the problem of mixed or impure motives we discussed at the beginning of the chapter.

The more we operate in this fallen state, the more we are enmeshed in something we cannot get out of. This rebelliousness is rooted in pride. It literally stinks to high heaven, for the one compelling reason that God cannot break into or through it to bring love to His creation.

In order to experience life with God, we must give up our pride. The good news is, God is there, by His Spirit, to help us to do that. But it still comes down to a choice. The Bible makes it very clear that humbling oneself is an essential act of moral will on the part of the individual. Examples abound: Christ humbled Himself to the point of dying on the cross, James says that we need to humble ourselves, the apostle Paul exhorts us to put on humility. It is a personal and deliberate act on our part as free moral agents; God waits for us and calls unto us to rid ourselves of the pride that separates us from relationship with Him.

In considering a world view and the right motives for approaching the lost with the gospel, it is important we operate on this level. Everything else involved in missions only makes sense, only has power to change lives, when the underlying theme is God's compassionate love, a love that is caring, unconditional, and forgiving. A love that is ours as a gift to receive and to live in; and a love which we are called to live out by demonstrating it to others.

God the Patient One:

We tend to think of the Old Testament as revealing a God who is harsh, punishing, and severe, while we think the New Testament reveals a God who may seem to have had a change of heart. This could not be further from the truth. Methodologies change, revelation progresses, and history unfolds, but God's character is constant. One of the prophets declares that God is the same today, yesterday and forever. His character is not fickle. There is no need for us to be insecure or unsure as to who we are dealing with when we are communicating with Him.

> Methodologies change, revelation progresses, and history unfolds, but God's character is constant.

That does not mean we don't struggle with that very problem. Sometimes it's as though there is a game going on to see whether "He loves me ... or ... He loves me not". But from the perspective of eternity, it's not open to question! When we come to God in prayer and commune with Him we can know for a certainty that whatever state we are in, whatever situation we are in, He is a compassionate and loving God. His acceptance of us is not dependent upon what we have done or thought, or on what we have accomplished or not accomplished! We might have to get some things right with Him and with others, but we are never rejected, never left alone by Him or excluded from Him, and never denied access into His presence. (You'll learn more about this later in this chapter, as we deal with the subject of condemnation.)

Someone once said that, as Christians, we need to keep short lists! That's what the atonement is all about (the suffering and accomplishment of Jesus on the cross). The apostle John says that we have an advocate with the Lord Jesus Christ; that if we sin and confess our sin to Him, we are forgiven. In the same vein, there is a story in the gospels where Peter asks Jesus how many times someone should forgive; Peter suggests the traditional view — seven times. Jesus, on the other hand, says we must forgive seven times seventy! There is no limit to forgiveness; there is no "forgiveness bank account" where, once the supply of forgiveness is all used up, then there is no use asking for more. God's forgiveness is always available; that's the model for us to follow, as well.

One very well-known passage of scripture serves to underscore this all important aspect to developing a proper world view; it appears at the end of the Lord's Prayer, which I believe Christ intended us to see as an outline of how the believer should pray and what he or she should include.

Jesus condemned those who were out to create fear of God, who wanted to develop a system of control through intimidation, and who marred the image of a loving and non-judgmental God

---

"Forgive us our sins as we forgive those who sin against us," is part and parcel of praying on a continual basis. In fact, Jesus declares that unless we forgive, our prayers will not be heard. So even serving the Lord, doing "stuff" for Him, or being a believer is drastically challenged when we live a life of unforgiveness, see God as an unforgiving God, or fail to make the central message of our lives in mission, one of forgiveness.

Paul the apostle says that as Christians, we carry this treasure in earthen vessels. The treasure is the mystery of God in Christ reconciling Himself to His creation through grace. We are literally a transportation device to carry the most powerful truth on the planet! The goal is to communicate this truth without adding to it or taking away from it or distorting it by thinking we have a better way, or by thinking someone else (person, organization, institution) knows a better way, or by sheer ignorance.

There is a story told of a theologian who on his death bed was visited by a journalist who asked one profound question. The learned theologian was asked what he felt was the most amazing truth he ever discovered through all the research, through all the learning, in all the books he had written over the course of his lifetime. The theologian's reply was, "Jesus loves me, this I know, for the Bible tells me so." It doesn't get much deeper than that; it doesn't get any more profound. When considering becoming a witness for Christ in our world today, your first step is to dig deep into yourself and consider your own belief system; journey into a life of knowing and living in God's love and compassion.

God who withholds judgment:

Another primary motive the believer must bring to their world view is an understanding of God's activity of withholding judgment. Too many religious or traditional concepts suggest that God is ready to pounce on people at every opportunity. In reality, God is constantly withholding judgment in hope that His grace and mercy will lead to repentance.

The Bible is packed with pictures of this wonderful God who withholds judgment in hope that His creation recognizes this act of mercy, and responds to His grace.

Translating this characteristic of God to communicating

the gospel to people means approaching them with total acceptance, and suspending accusation, criticism, and condemnation.

That may surprise you. You may, in fact, believe that our mission involves a message of accusation, criticism and condemnation. Isn't that part of our story?

Absolutely not! If you read the Gospels without the colored lens of religion you will quickly see that Jesus condemned people who carried out exactly that kind of mission. He condemned those who were out to create fear of God, who wanted to develop a system of control through intimidation, and who marred the image of a loving and non-judgmental God. The gospel clearly teaches a message that is called the "good news"!

To the readers of his day it was a very clear message of a God who was personal, relational, approachable, and who came to put His stamp of approval on His creation by becoming like His creation.

We see in Jesus a ministry that did not condemn but literally freed people from the bondage and fear of an impending wrath that would ultimately end in destruction. When I am teaching on this subject, I always ask the group to quote John 3:16; most, if not all, know the verse. However, when invited to quote the very next verse, only a small percentage know it and even fewer understand it. John 3:17 follows on the wonderful declaration of God loving and giving with a revelation of His ultimate motive. That motive is that He did not come to bring condemnation but to offer life. How many times have we brought the message of condemnation in place of the message of life to others? How many of us live under a message of condemnation in place of living under a message of life?

Paul the apostle declares that there is no condemnation to those who are in Christ Jesus. The word "condemnation" means to demean or devalue the worth of a person or thing. Jesus came to affirm His love for His creation and communicate its fantastic worth. John says that Jesus, as "the Word," became one of us and dwelt among us. What did John mean? To the readers of his day it was a very clear message of a God who was personal, relational, approachable, and who came to put His stamp of approval on His creation by becoming like His creation.

That may seem like a mouthful, but take a few minutes to muse or meditate on that truth. It will rock your world! Still trying to understand the accuracy of this truth? Let me help out by contrasting the difference between condemnation — which is not a part of God's message — and conviction — which is a part of God's message.

"Condemnation" is the devaluing of a person or thing. God is not into that and does not intend for us to understand Him on these terms.

"Conviction," which is part of the message as we find in John's Gospel, is one of the roles of the Holy Spirit and is illustrated in events Jesus was involved with during His ministry on earth. We see conviction played out in Acts chapter two, after Peter's Day of Pentecost sermon, when the people hearing the message were "cut to their heart." They were so convicted by what Peter had to say they felt they needed to do something about it. Peter told them to confess their sin, repent, be baptized and receive the Holy Spirit.

There is so much packed into this one event that volumes and volumes could be written about it. Essentially, what happened on that day was, thousands of people received Jesus Christ as their personal Lord and Savior as a result of a strong conviction coming upon them. It's important to realize that this was conviction, not a sense of condemnation that would have made them run or hide from shame. When Adam and Eve sinned, a sense of shame overcame them and when God called out to meet them they hid or ran away from His presence.

Conviction, in contrast, is the awareness and realization that someone greater is present and is wholly other and awesome. This realization or awareness leads to voluntary change and humility. Instead of sensing the ever-present shame that makes us want to run away, there is a compelling appeal to draw close to God.

In developing a world view it is essential that we really grasp and understand this part of God's wonderful plan of salvation. As Paul the apostle says, any other gospel is not a genuine gospel. Our message in mission is that God is loving, compassionate, and a judgment-withholding God.

The ultimate display of God's compassion and love is depicted in Jesus dying on the cross for our sins. It is the centerpiece of the Christian belief system and of our faith. As Paul says, if Christ is not raised from the dead then we are of all people to be pitied. In John 3:16 we read the message of the gospel in the most compelling manner. "God so loved the world that He gave His only begotten Son that whoever would believe in Him would not die but have everlasting life."

Every aspect of this key passage of scripture is important, including the actual grammar. The subject is God Himself, what He is and what He does. God loves whosoever and God gives His Son to die. This verse also declares the unconditional aspect of the act; it was an initiative taken that was not based on any previous event. God was not responding to something we had done. He started it all. God in His love just gave His Son. We also discover that the intended recipients were "whosoevers" — not a certain people, ethnic group, race, or religion.

Once again, the motive for missions and the world view that is needed is one whose subject is God, not anything else; and one whose object is whosoever. We all tend to carry with us biases that create filters. When we approach people or groups, these filters prevent us from presenting the clear gospel. The motive in which we operate must flow from a realization that we are all "whosoevers," as undeserving of salvation as the person next to us. What we pass on is the joy we have received, not the conditions we place on the gospel.

...the motive for missions and the world view that is needed is one whose subject is God, not anything else; and one whose object is whosoever.

Summary:

In order to properly approach missions and in order to communicate with others about the grace of God, we first must be the recipients of this same grace. We see the clarity of the word "love" and the force with which Jesus communicates His unconditional love. It is important for us to pray for that same unconditional love to share with others and for ourselves to experience it as well. Alignment to God's approach to others who are in need of His grace and mercy will allow us to reflect something that will capture the imagination and heart of those who hear this message.

Because we are all susceptible to erroneous concepts of God's love it is important to be called back to the basis of understanding — God desires to free us, forgive us, and share Himself with us in intimacy. The God who we serve is patient, forgiving, merciful, compassionate, and unconditional in acceptance and love. To know this about Him is to walk and live in a wholly other dimension; it is this place from which we are able to invite others into this same wholly other dimension. The Christian manifesto for the missionary is the proclamation of the freeing truth set forth above. It is nothing new, but the old time Gospel that we must continually call ourselves back to, because of the never ending wandering we are subject to as fallen creatures. All we like sheep stray!

At the end of the day, missions and communicating the gospel cross culturally entails understanding intellectually, and knowing experientially who God is. The identifications of who God revealed Himself as in the books of the Bible are a beginning.

In Genesis, He is the Creator God.

In Exodus, He is the Redeemer.

In Leviticus, He is your Sanctifier.

In Numbers, He is your Guide.

In Deuteronomy, He is your Teacher.

In Joshua, He is the Mighty Conqueror.

In Judges, He gives victory over enemies.

In Ruth, He is your Kinsman, your Lover, and your Redeemer.

In 1 Samuel, He is the Root of Jesse.

In 2 Samuel, He is the Son of David.

In 1 and 2 Kings, He is King of Kings and Lord of Lords.

In 1 and 2 Chronicles, He is your Intercessor and High Priest.

In Ezra, He is your temple, your house of worship.

In Nehemiah, He is your mighty wall, protecting you from your enemies.

In Esther, He stands in the gap to deliver you from your enemies.

In Job, He is the Arbitrator who not only understands your struggles, but has the power to do something about them.

In Psalms, He is your Song — and your reason to sing.

In Proverbs, He is your wisdom, helping you make sense of life and live it successfully.

In Ecclesiastes, He is your purpose, delivering you from vanity.

In the Song of Solomon, He is your Lover, your Rose of Sharon.

In Isaiah, He is the Mighty Counselor, the Prince of Peace, the Everlasting Father, and more. In short, He's everything you need.

In Jeremiah, He is your Balm in Gilead, the soothing salve for your sin-sick soul.

In Lamentations, He is the ever-faithful One upon Whom you can depend.

In Ezekiel, He is your Wheel in the middle of a wheel — the One who assures that dry, dead bones will come alive again.

In Daniel, He is the Ancient of Days, the everlasting God who never runs out of time.

In Hosea, He is your Faithful Lover, always beckoning you to come back — when you have abandoned Him.

In Joel, He is your Refuge, keeping you safe in times of trouble.

In Amos, He is the Husbandman, the One you can depend on to stay by your side.

In Obadiah, He is Lord of the Kingdom.

In Jonah, He is your Salvation, bringing you back within His will.

In Micah, He is Judge of the nation.

In Nahum, He is the jealous God.

In Habakkuk, He is the Holy One.

In Zephaniah, He is the Witness.

In Haggai, He overthrows the enemies.

In Zechariah, He is Lord of Hosts.
In Malachi, He is Merciful.
In Matthew, He is King of the Jews.
In Mark, He is the Servant.
In Luke, He is the Son of Man, feeling what you feel.
In John, He is the Son of God.
In Acts, He is the Savior of the world.
In Romans, He is the righteousness of God.
In 1 Corinthians, He is the Rock that followed Israel.
In 2 Corinthians, He is the Triumphant One, giving victory.
In Galatians, He is your liberty; He sets you free.
In Ephesians, He is Head of the Church.
In Philippians, He is your joy.
In Colossians, He is your completeness.
In 1 and 2 Thessalonians, He is your hope.
In 1 Timothy, He is your faith.
In 2 Timothy, He is your stability.
In Philemon, He is your Benefactor.
In Titus, He is Truth.
In Hebrews, He is your perfection.
In James, he is the Power behind your faith.
In 1 Peter, He is your example.
In 2 Peter, He is your purity.
In 1 John, He is your life.
In 2 John, He is your pattern.
In 3 John, He is your motivation.
In Jude, He is the foundation of your faith.
In Revelation, He is your coming King.

Source unknown

CHAPTER TWO

A Biblical Foundation for a World View

The early nineties brought many new and exciting opportunities for the church to engage in missions. The Berlin Wall had come crumbling down, Communism was now defunct as a significant force in the world, and the Iron Curtain gave way to a great unveiling of freedom. During this time, our mission institutes were being prepared to go into Eastern Europe, to establish relationships with the churches there and work alongside them to spread the Gospel.

As our team traveled through Russia, on to Ukraine, and

finally into Rumania, we had the thrill of experiencing, first hand, the tearing down of the old forms of government and the installation of new ones. In Ukraine we woke up one morning to be escorted to the very first day of operations of the head office for the Pentecostal Churches in that country, after seventy years of Communist rule. To this day, when I look at the picture taken of those church leaders and our team, it engenders all kinds of emotion within me. Passing through the middle of the city, we saw thousands of people celebrating in a square. They were dismantling a statue of Lenin and changing the name of the square from Revolution Square to Freedom Square. It would not be the last statue representing the former Communist government we would see being torn down, nor the last renaming of a building or place.

During this trip the team ran into quite a hostile situation while on the train from Hungary to Rumania. The guards and police were still very nervous and skeptical about foreigners coming into their country. Tired, hungry, and in much need of connecting with someone we would know who would assist us on the next leg of our missions trip, we were confronted instead by very aggressive guards demanding all sorts of things from us in a language we didn't understand. At two in the morning in a different country, all of us being very tired, it played out like something from an espionage movie. But it was real and it was serious. We didn't know what to do, nor were we prepared for such a confrontation.

Then, just as they were moving into our little room on the train to begin confiscating our luggage, I remembered a very wise and forward-thinking member of our team who was traveling with the containers we had sent on ahead. That person had made sure I carried with me a complete list of contents itemized in the Rumanian language and bearing the official seal of the government counsel. I began to make some noise and reached back for my briefcase; I knew I was taking the risk that they might think I was taking a hostile action; I did not know if that would spell out some extremely negative consequences.

But as I flashed the documents in front of the guards, they recognized, not the contents list nor any statement of the wonderful work we were going to do in their country, but the government seal. Once they saw something official, we were off the hook. During the rest of our time there, that document came in handy for many things.

This chapter is about the believers' government seal given by God for the work we do cross culturally. Paul the apostle lists several values in the following portion of Scripture that shift our presentation to the world from one that is bland and ordinary to one of significant purpose and blessing.

2 Corinthians 5:1-6:13 (RSV):

"For we know that if the earthly tent we live in is destroyed, we have a building from God, a house not made with hands, eternal in the heavens. Here indeed we groan, and long to put on our heavenly dwelling, so that by putting it on we may not be found naked. For while we are still in this tent, we sigh with anxiety; not that we would be unclothed, but that we would be further clothed, so that what is mortal may be swallowed up by life. He who has prepared us for this very thing is God, who has given us the Spirit as a guarantee.

"So we are always of good courage; we know that while we are at home in the body we are away from the Lord, for we walk by faith, not by sight. We are of good courage, and we would rather be away from the body and at home with the Lord. So whether we are at home or away, we make it our aim to please Him. For we must all appear before the judgment seat of Christ, so that each one may receive good or evil, according to what he has done in the body.

"Therefore, knowing the fear of the Lord, we persuade men; but what we are is known to God, and I hope it is known also to your conscience. We are not commending ourselves to you again but giving you cause to be proud of us, so that you may be able to answer those who pride themselves on a man's position and not on his heart. For if we are beside ourselves, it is for God; if we are in our right mind, it is for you. For the love of Christ controls us, because we are convinced that one has died for all; therefore all have died. And He died for all, that those who live might live no longer for themselves but for Him who for their sake died and was raised.

"From now on, therefore, we regard no one from a human point of view; even though we once regarded Christ from a human point of view, we regard Him thus no longer. Therefore, if any one is in Christ, he is a new creation; the old has passed away, behold, the new has come. All this is from God, who through Christ reconciled us to Himself and gave us the ministry of reconciliation; that is, in Christ God was reconciling the world to Himself, not counting their trespasses against them, and entrusting to us the message of reconciliation. So we are ambassadors for Christ, God making His appeal through us. We beseech you on behalf of Christ, be reconciled to God. For our sake He made Him to be sin who knew no sin, so that in Him we might become the righteousness of God.

"Working together with Him, then, we entreat you not to accept the grace of God in vain. For He says, 'At the acceptable time I have listened to you, and helped you on the day of salvation.' Behold, now is the acceptable time; behold, now is the day of salvation. We put no obstacle in any one's way, so that no fault may be found with our ministry, but as servants of God we commend ourselves in every way: through great endurance, in afflictions, hardships, calamities, beatings, imprisonments, tumults, labors, watching, hunger; by purity, knowledge, forbearance, kindness, the Holy Spirit, genuine love, truthful speech, and the power of God; with the weapons of righteousness for the right hand and for the left; in honor and dishonor, in ill repute and good repute. We are treated as impostors, and yet are true; as unknown, and yet well known; as dying, and behold we live; as punished, and yet not killed; as sorrowful, yet always rejoicing; as poor, yet making many rich; as having nothing, and yet possessing everything. Our mouth is open to you, Corinthians; our heart is wide. You are not restricted by us, but you are restricted in your own affections. In return — I speak as to children — widen your hearts also."

The love of Christ controls us:

Perhaps we could say the Corinthian church had it half right. A commentator I once read said the Corinthian church was in the world as it needs to be, but the world was in the church as it shouldn't be.

The city of Corinth had all the ingredients a typical, cosmopolitan city of that day would have had. It even sounds familiar, today. Corinth had a plurality of religious beliefs, a multicultural makeup, diverse industry and trade, and a highly competitive climate.

Put another way, the people of this city were clearly in need of a proper Christian world view! A church was planted in Corinth, a church that reflected the same diverse, cosmopolitan flavor as the city itself. It must have been an exciting place, with a large congregation, dynamic leadership, and an abundance of supernatural gifts in operation.

However, there were other problems that rose primarily from the competitive nature of the pervasive culture; this led to the development of factions in the church. These factions, which surrounded the differing personalities of the leadership, soon led to hostile resentment, aggressive posturing for position, and outright arrogance in the church. The leadership even took to criticizing the apostle Paul. Paul was quick to respond to the criticism; his letters to the Christians of Corinth are now two key books in our New Testament. He pulled no punches in seeking to help bring correction to the Corinthian church.

In chapter five of his second letter to the church, Paul laid out the proper world view for a Christian. Here we find a concise and clear outline of the elements that go into the approach the believer needs to have in order to become effective in missions.

The controlling factor:

The first point Paul makes is a reflection of his own motive for embarking on his missions trip from Israel to Greece. He explained it clearly and simply: the love of Christ controlled his life now; Paul no longer sought to be in charge, himself.

The question is, what is our bottom line? Is Jesus just a good suggestion? Is the Great Commission just an option? Or is Jesus truly the Way, and the Great Commission God's first priority?

Paul had once been in bondage to a religion; he had invested all his activity and emotion in that religion, until he had an encounter with Christ that turned his world upside down (that is, upside right!). The pinnacle of this upheaval came while he traveled on the road to Damascus with written consent to have Christians arrested and put into jail. (This was not his first such mission; Paul was also a consenting witness to Stephen's martyrdom.) But en route to Damascus, Jesus Himself appeared to Paul and a marvellous, miraculous turn-around occurred.

A great commission was placed upon Paul's life. Part of this commission was to travel the world, reaching out to a people he once despised and proclaiming the love of Jesus that he now had experienced. As a matter of fact it was this very love that he was to proclaim.

When Paul says that the love of Christ controls him, he is referring to the historical act of Jesus on the cross. The tremendous love of God, expressed in that event, was what captivated Paul until his dying day. Someone once referred to Paul as "the cross-eyed preacher" because of the consistency of his message of the cross. Any motives, any thoughts, any opinions, any desires he may have had were all subjected to the one compelling reason for living — the love of Christ.

When we are considering our motives for mission, it is crucial that the "bottom line," the foundation, be established. It's called "a reason for being" and without it all options are left hanging open and the clear message is lost. Whether it be in business, family, politics, or religion, if there is not a clear reason or motive to do something, then we can easily find ourselves embracing any other option that comes by. Paul didn't have this problem — he didn't consider any alternatives for the rest of his life after that day on the road to Damascus and his close encounter with Christ. Paul was set free from hate and religion and now was free to serve Christ and to serve other human beings. He never deviated from that bottom line motive.

The question is, what is our bottom line? Is Jesus just a good suggestion? Is the Great Commission just an option? Or is Jesus truly the Way, and the Great Commission God's first priority? If so, our aligning to Him and to His Great Commission is essential if we are to be effective world Christians. Again we see, as in Chapter One, that motive is the essential ingredient of service in the Christian life.

Seeing people as allies ... not as the enemy:

Paul was a man without prejudice. He called us to set aside our human presumptions, our prejudices, our biases, and look at people as Christ looks at them. This man had the religious pedigree of an Olympic champion; he rose ahead of his class, he proved himself superior to his peers in many ways, he was born and nurtured in the best of conditions. And here, he laid all that aside, and claimed to have learned a different way of looking at people.

He went so far as to say that he saw people through the cross. Christ died for their sins and thus they are as qualified as he to inherit the Kingdom of God. This is definitely not the old Paul (then known as Saul) who immediately excluded anyone who did not fit his paradigm of spirituality.

Today, in our enthusiasm, we can easily exclude others from enjoying the same freedom we claim to have. In our sincerity and excitement over what we have experienced, we feel that anyone who does not quite have the same experience as we do is just not right with God! So we embark on a mission to get people to experience, feel, and act like us; this becomes more important to us than the desire to communicate the truth of Jesus Christ and having Him do the inner work through the Holy Spirit.

The fact is, what God does in someone else's life may not look like your experience! And truthfully, given our tendency to impose our own experience on God's plan, this may not be such a bad thing.

The key point is — the truth sets free; the point is not that the truth produces identical experiences. In our day, especially, it often seems that the truth we are to proclaim is at the mercy of the experience we are having. It is a sad day for the church when we seem more concerned about how people manifest or act in a certain way and less concerned about the passion to convey the love of Christ.

Not only does Paul come out and declare the importance of viewing people through the lens of Christ's perspective but he states that to minister effectively, we all must have this perspective. It was said of William Booth, the founder of the Salvation Army, that as he walked by a drunken derelict lying in the street, he proclaimed, "there go I but for the grace of God!" People who are captivated by the love of Christ see others differently. People are not "those sinners," but are lost brothers and sisters for whom Christ has already died, who need to come to a full realization of that truth. A biblical world view will be one in which we see people through the cross of Christ and not through our own prejudices.

Paul goes on to say something that is rather perplexing. After stating that a world view consists of seeing people differently than we once did, he adds that we even see Christ differently.

A "world view" is something every person on this planet carries with him or her. Our world view is composed of learned and experienced reference points assimilated from parents, siblings, friends, teachers, cultures, and the like; these form the grid through which we see life.

> A biblical world view will be one in which we see people through the cross of Christ and not through our own prejudices.

The Bible reveals the world view of Jesus and other biblical characters, the same world view that we ourselves are to embrace. It will encompass such things as belief in the supernatural; life beyond the grave; an accounting for all we do here on earth; the existence of evil and its powers; a God who is creator of all things; the conviction Jesus was God; the life, death, and resurrection of Jesus; the work of the Holy Spirit in a person's life; and the need for individuals to accept Christ as Savior. All these are components of a biblical world view.

Just as others walk with a "window" on the world, so do we. The biblical teachings are that window which affects every aspect of our lives and every decision we make.

However, just like the Corinthian church, we are all susceptible to allowing the influence of external conditions to mold us. In his letter to the church at Rome, Paul challenges Christians to not be conformed to the image of this world but to be conformed to the likeness of Christ.

> Our world view is so ingrained within us that it takes constant application of the new world view (in our case a biblical world view) in our lives to bring about the internal changes that allow us to really begin to change our behavior.

At this moment I am typing this on my computer. Technologists will tell you that as I use my computer, the hard drive keeps an image of all activities: the files saved, the applications installed, the internet sites visited. If someone had the skills and the proper tools they could see this activity image I have created on my hard drive and give you a pretty accurate profile of who I am. No matter who I claim to be, a computer whiz could probably reveal the truth.

After a short-term missions summit I hosted recently, everyone in attendance took a tour through a federal government computer refurbishing plant. One of the most interesting insights during our time in the 40,000 square foot plant was that, in order to get down to the "cleanest" hard drive possible, the technicians were required to erase seven levels of data from every hard drive that came in to be refurbished. That is to say, computer technicians have the capability to discover data on a hard drive up to seven layers deep! So, when you "reformat" your drive, thinking it's like new, think again. There are levels of data that can still be exposed!

We're something like those hard drives. Our world view is so ingrained within us that it takes constant application of the new world view (in our case a biblical world view) in our lives to bring about the internal changes that allow us to really begin to change our behavior.

Jesus is Lord

The disciples were traveling with Jesus one day when He asked them a very pointed question: "Who do men say that I am?"

Jesus was always interested in people and their perceptions. After all, He came to this world entirely because of His love for each and all of us. Peter began listing the various views about who Jesus might really be. Some said He was Moses or Elijah come back from the dead. Some thought He was some other great prophet. Others said He was a great teacher or good person. Some even said He was Satan!

When all the feedback was in, Jesus asked the disciples who they thought He was. Peter responded on behalf of the disciples, saying they thought He was the Christ (the Anointed One). Jesus' response to this was to tell the disciples that flesh and blood had not revealed this to them but the Spirit of God. In other words, the revelation to people of who Jesus is, is a spiritual act initiated by God Himself.

This is very good news for us in our mission. We do not need to try to convince or prove Jesus to others. That is God's job, through His Spirit.

This is not to say there is no room for arguing the case for Christianity, but it is to say that at some point, an act of the Holy Spirit needs to occur whereby a person comes to the realization that Jesus is the Lord and Savior of humanity. This critical, life-transforming moment needs to take place in order to seal the deal!

Today there are religions and cults which claim that Jesus is a part of their belief system and that He plays a very significant role. However, when one probes further down, it becomes evident that in the world view of these groups, Jesus is someone very different from who He claimed to be, who the disciples said He was, or who the early church worshiped as Lord.

When Paul refers to believers not seeing Christ from a human point of view anymore, he is saying that we cannot redefine Jesus according to our own personal view, we cannot mold our personal Christ into our chosen image, but that we are acknowledging Him for who He really is, the Lord of our lives. "Lord," in biblical times, was a term everyone understood. "Lord" was the title the rulers of that day used, to refer to themselves. To call someone "Lord" was to claim that individual had absolute authority over you, had ownership of your life.

When the early Christians claimed Jesus as Lord, the governmental authorities understood what a threat that was to their power. They persecuted the Christians for disloyalty to the government; they called them traitors! A biblical world view is one in which claiming Jesus as Lord (absolute authority and complete owner) is essential. Any other concept, perception or attitude was unacceptable in biblical times and continues to be unacceptable to this day. Paul tells believers in Philippians that, "every knee will bow and every tongue will confess that Jesus is Lord." That is the posture of the believer, to claim here and now that Jesus is Lord, that He is the one with absolute authority and complete ownership of our lives.

C.S. Lewis once suggested that only two religions would exist in the end times. One would be Christianity, the other, Hinduism. He said the former would exist due to its exclusivist position on Jesus being the only way to Heaven, and the latter due to its inclusive position that there are many ways to Nirvana.

Whether Lewis got it right as to which world religion would be standing alongside Christianity is not the point here (there may be one, or several). The point is in the stand we take, as Christians, as to our loyalty to the leader of our faith, Jesus. Jesus is either who He says He is, or He is not. Christians, from the disciples first until today, have lived and died by the foundational faith that Jesus was telling the truth. That claim, and our response to it, produces the perception of others concerning our commitment to Jesus and who Jesus is.

…we cannot redefine Jesus according to our own
personal view, we cannot mold our
personal Christ into our chosen image,
but that we are acknowledging Him for who
He really is, the Lord of our lives.

Paul — an extreme religious loyalist who sought to imprison and destroy followers of Christ because they were traitors to his religion — was radically altered in his world view by an encounter with the living Christ. He ended up understanding in the light of that love that Christianity was not mean-spirited nor some aristocratic sect, but indeed good news for all mankind. Our stance for Christ should not separate us out in a way that shows condemnation toward others; our stance for Christ should make us lights that attract others.

All too often we either take a passive position for fear of intimidation, or an aggressive position in which our Christianity comes across as elitist, treating people with contempt. But if you re-read the Gospels, you will find that is not the approach of Jesus. The only ones who were targets of his criticism were the religious leaders of his day who operated from false motives of control.

We Are new creations:

The next characteristic of a Christian world view, according to Paul in 2 Corinthians 5, is that if anyone is in Christ they are a new creature and that the past is done away with. This revitalization of a person's spirit when he or she is born again is permanent and constant. When we accept Christ, everything we have ever done, any sin we have ever committed, is dealt with. Christ, on the cross and through His resurrection, took away our sin, forgave us, and restored our broken relationship with God. We literally become new creations of God.

In a day and age when there is such a great psychological emphasis on "going deeper," and "working through" our past issues, the Bible knows only one thing. We are forgiven, we are washed in the blood of Christ and we have a "new lease" on life. Do believers still have issues? Do they still need a deeper more profound experience with God? Of course! However, we must also keep in mind that Christ did all the work for us on the cross and that we have a new standing with God, a new relationship with Him and a new future with Him.

Paul goes on to tell us in another part of the letter to the Corinthians that "we were washed, we were cleansed, and we were saved" from our past. What does this have to do with developing a world view? Why is this such an important concept to understand for a world view? It's important because, as humans, we naturally tend to limit ourselves or diminish the effect of the cross, and in turn we pass on to others the same inefficient understanding of the power of the cross and its transforming power.

Paul understood the transforming power of the cross. He

understood grace; and he also understood the call to live a transformed life. This is why he was persecuted as a Christian; this is the limb that he went out on, which others had such a difficult time understanding.

A biblical world view is one in which claiming Jesus as Lord (absolute authority and complete owner) is essential.

In the last chapter of his letter to the Galatians, Paul calls the church to complete trust in "the cross of our Lord Jesus Christ." He urges believers to celebrate Christ, and to cease depending on works of the flesh. The problem in Galatia was that some of the leaders of the church were trying to combine traditional signs of faith — circumcision, for example — with the newfound freedom in Christ. Forget it, said Paul. Leave tradition and the law behind, and revel in the freedom of Christ, even if this brings criticism, or — as in his own case — actual persecution. Paul says he bears the marks of persecution of Christ — and still glories only in the cross of Christ.

Paul also recognizes that this new freedom from works can be misunderstood, and so he explains (Romans 6) that we must not use freedom in Christ as an excuse to feel free to sin. He knows that the radical new position of freedom begs the question whether we can continue sinning and living the way we used to if we are completely "off the hook."

As free moral agents, each believer has the freedom in Christ to live the way he or she wants. But as followers of Christ, why would we want to live in a way that does not honor Him? As Paul says in Corinthians, "all things are permissible, but not all things are expedient." The freedom of the cross allows the believer to live, say, and act in anyway they desire. But Paul's unshakable conviction is that the love of Christ is so compelling that the natural reaction of the believer is to be so overwhelmed by Jesus that he or she will want to submit to Him to the point that they will only want to become a servant and live a life of obedience.

> The world view that we are to carry in us as Christians is one where there is a renewed image of who we are as God's creation.

If you have ever asked yourself, "What's so radical about Christianity?" — this is it! You meet a God who is so trusting and secure that He frees His creation to make free-will choices that He believes will result in a new relationship with Him that translates into people becoming a new creation.

As new creations, we automatically reflect to others the power of the cross and we trust that this will lead to a desire in those around us to want what we have; that this will open doors of opportunity to share Christ in such a way that they will want to put their trust in Christ as well. Paul also told the Corinthians that we are "living letters of Christ." Our lives are the greatest witness, testimony, and message of Christ. The questions is, how is your life witness? How is mine?

The world view that we are to carry in us as Christians is one where there is a renewed image of who we are as God's creation. So often we operate with a sense of false humility, which is of no use to others, the Kingdom of God, or ourselves. From the very beginning we were created in God's image. Sin entered in and marred this image, but with Christ transforming us through the cross, that image has been restored. The Christian life should not be a path to self-improvement, but a life of discovery of how much we have in Christ.

A Biblical Foundation for a World view

We are ambassadors:

In this chapter, Paul deals with another important biblical foundation for a Christian world view — being an ambassador for Christ. Most of us understand what an ambassador is; however, it is something else again to realize that we, ourselves, are commissioned as ambassadors. And not merely for a secular state — we are ambassadors for Christ!

Recently a G-8 summit had just ended in Kannaskis, Alberta, Canada. This is a meeting of world leaders who come together to discuss issues of a global nature. Presidents and Prime Ministers from the United States, Canada, England, France, Russia, Italy, Japan and Germany, along with many other dignitaries from those countries, come together to share ideas and concepts, and to attempt to come to some resolution as to how best address world economic challenges. Each country is carefully and thoughtfully prepared to state their position on these issues and also, of course, to present themselves in the best possible light. They are all acting as ambassadors for their respective countries.

The Bible states that as believers, we are citizens of heaven, and that we represent that Kingdom... the Kingdom of Heaven; the Kingdom of God. Many believers feel overwhelmed at discovering the will of God; many others are frantically trying to discover the will of God for their lives. We are challenged, exhorted, told by leaders, churches, and friends we need to find the will of God for our lives.

But let's just relax for a moment. The Bible is already clear on what God's will is. Wherever we are, whenever the time is appropriate, whoever is available, we are to be an ambassador for Christ. Our job is the same as that of the dignitaries who attended the G-8 Summit to represent the kingdom of God at all times.

But it's worth noting that the first thing those G-8 representatives did, was to leave their home countries to attend the gathering. The challenge before us as believers is to move out from the "sanctuary mentality" of gathering for our own spiritual benefit, and move to the New Testament mentality that understands every believer carries this treasure in earthen vessels and is commissioned to express faith in their community and in their world!

If this concept is difficult to understand, maybe it will become clearer if we move onto the next point in Paul's message on having a Christian world view.

Book keeping and the Gospel:

At the time I am writing this book, some shocking and serious revelations have come out concerning the mismanagement of funds in some of the largest and most respected companies in the United States. In short (very short), the books are not lining up as they should and people are going to go to prison for it. The magnitude of these discoveries may be historical, but the existence of accounting "discrepancies" is not.

In fact, Christians have always been called to be ministers of balancing books. What do I mean by that?

Immediately after making his point on ambassadorship, Paul says that we have a ministry of reconciliation. "Reconciliation" is a common Greek word used in biblical times; it means "to balance the books." When an accountant works on someone's finances, the primary function is to track the inflow and outflow of money, compare income to the expenses incurred, and see if they balance out or if money was made or lost. The comparison then is "reconciled" or "justified," in order to bring a balance to the financial accounts.

In most world religions, reconciliation with God is believed to come from a deep and profound commitment to the teaching and rituals of that particular religion. In the case of Paul's religion, the practice was to attempt to balance out the wrongs against God with a lot of good acts or rigorous keeping of the

Law and all the particular rules and regulations that had been created over time. The Greek mystery religions that were very popular in Paul's time had a perilous belief that their god was angry and all kinds of sacrifices and duties had to be performed in order to appease this anger.

> "Reconciliation" is a common Greek word used in biblical times; it means "to balance the books."

Paul understands that we indeed need to be reconciled with God. But he also knew that the balance could never be achieved — our sin is simply too great to be balanced off with good works or religious ritual.

But Paul knew that we did not need to accomplish this reconciliation through our own efforts. He saw the work of Christ on the cross as doing just that with us in our sin. We in our sin owed a debt to God that was payable with our very lives. The consequences of our choosing to reject God and live on our own were such that eternal death was our future. However, Jesus took our debt of sin to God when He was on the cross. effectively creating a balance in our "sin to debt ratio". Jesus reconciled or balanced our account with God, allowing relationship to be restored.

This is the good news of the Gospel, and the message and activity that needs to fill the believer's life on earth. The good news is that someone paid the debt we owed and which we could never pay off. The activity is to involve our lives in communicating this message to others who have not heard the good news, or have been ignoring it and need to respond to this powerful truth.

So, you see — to discover God's will, to find a purpose, and to figure out what needs to be said is actually very simple. I fear that our current Christian culture focuses on attempting to challenge people with discovering their destiny, achieving more prominence, and moving up the ladder of spiritually gifted effectiveness. But what God really wants is faithful and available followers who will share with others the powerful truth of His Son's action on the cross. We are to share, with whoever will listen, the amazing fact that our lives have been reconciled to God and that theirs can be also.

Complicated? No.
Confusing? No.
Powerful? Yes.

...what God really wants is faithful and available
followers who will share with others
the powerful truth of His Son's action on the cross.

A sense of community is another important piece in becoming a Christian with a world view. At the end of 2 Corinthians, we read that Jesus, who knew no sin, became sin for us so the we might become the righteousness (be in right standing) of God. The content of our message is the story of what God did in Jesus and what personally has happened to us.

Everyone who claims a relationship with Christ has a story to tell. In a world in which the predominant world view is one of either ignoring the fact of an eternal destiny that must be confronted, or a world view where a positive eternal destiny is based upon the good and hard work of the individual (which is futile), our proclamation is that there is another option! That is, choosing Jesus as Savior and accepting the accomplished work of the cross. Our message is of an action already done for each and every person ever born or yet to be born on this planet!

The unity factor:

Paul draws our attention to our need, as believers, to understand the nature of being workers "together" in God's plan of salvation. The Corinthian church had a major competition problem, stemming from deeply rooted issues embedded right in the DNA of the city. As hosts of the Isthmian Games, which were a prelude to the Olympic Games, a very hot and competitive nature was inbred in the people. This created divisions and hostilities among the different groups in the city and even spilled over into the church.

This is what motivated Paul to write to the church in the beginning, as we see in 1 Corinthians chapter one. Obviously this was not the true reflection of the body of Christ, nor a reflection of what was to happen when salvation visited a group of people. Paul reminds them that they have a common purpose and goal that needs to become the "unity factor" in their behavior. That purpose and goal was to spread the message of Christ becoming sin, so that we could become the righteousness of God.

Paul also states that this work cannot be accomplished in a competitive or divisive way, but only by demonstrating the unity that Christ brings. In John 17, we find Jesus' prayer to His Father just before His trial, arrest, and death on the cross. As we read His prayer, we discover that the heart's desire of Jesus and of His Father was that the disciples — and those who came to believe as a result of their mission — would be one, as They are one. Christians are to be as united in love as are God the Father, God the Son, and God the Holy Spirit.

When one considers that the last words of a dying person should tend to be among the most significant words someone would utter, the importance of this emphasis on unity is highlighted even further. I cannot tell you how many international mission trips I have participated in — as a member, leader or organizer — whose success has been based on the unity of the mission team more than on what was done or said.

I once heard speaker say that people are tired of Christians telling them to believe the gospel while those Christians are not behaving the gospel. Notice the emphasis here! Maybe when we begin behaving the gospel, bringing into practice Jesus' prayer that we would be one, then the world will take notice and begin to believe the gospel.

Much of Jesus' teaching about relationship is summed up in the Beatitudes, found in the Gospel of Matthew. I often wonder where the Beatitudes have gone in all the differing "flavors of the month" buzz words in the church today. A truly biblical world view will be demonstrated in a lifestyle of community and unity.

Our hearts the central message:

The last thing in this chapter that Paul draws our attention to with regards to developing a Christian world view is living an open life.

After sharing his agonizing and sometimes painful experiences, Paul urges the believers of the Corinthian church to, "open their hearts wide" to him. He states that he has been open with them, has laid out the proper world view they are to have, and has been vulnerable with them; now he asks that they do the same.

If the church is to survive today, let alone thrive and share the gospel, it must learn to trust and be open. Someone once said that openness begets openness. As believers we must take the initiative to be open and honest with others and to risk sharing our very lives. When humanity fell from God, relationship was broken; we have craved relationship ever since. In fact, so desperately have we craved relationship that we have been willing to compromise our own dignity and settle for debasing, demeaning relationships to try to fill the void. But inevitably, we come to regret it in the end; our failed efforts result in destruction to others and ourselves. We destroy our own lives and the lives of others by attempting to fill this deep void within us that only Jesus Christ can fill.

One of the most compelling street dramas our mission teams performed was called "The Empty Heart". It is a very powerful and relevant drama because it speaks of the human predicament in all of us. A clown comes onto the stage with a huge box shaped like a heart stuck on his chest. The lid opens up and different people come along, holding different things, each promising that they are able to fill the empty heart of the clown. One after the other the clown gladly takes their offers, hoping to be satisfied. The first gift is flowers representing sexual love, the second is money, the next drugs and alcohol, the next something of a material nature, then finally something representing religion.

The clown attempts to fill his empty heart with all the things people try to use to fill their empty hearts; his efforts come to nothing. The attempts each end in failure.

Then the scene turns to Jesus on the cross, dying. He comes off the Cross and gives to the clown His very own heart; it's a perfect fit. The clown kneels down in adoration and appreciation and the two walk off together in relationship.

…people are tired of Christians telling them to believe the gospel while those Christians are not behaving the gospel.

The greatest expression of salvation is the restored relationship with God and with one another; that's the good news to a world that has an empty heart and is attempting to fill it with all kinds of destructive things. The unity we show, along with the purity of relationship that builds up and affirms, is the calling card of the church.

Summary:

Unless we as Christians learn the secrets of developing an effective world view — the world view we are taught by the apostle Paul — we are in double danger. First, we risk missing the whole point of salvation ourselves, and second we are in danger of passing on to others a toxic concept of Christianity that can lead to rejection of the message or a watered down version of the real thing. The only way to prevent this is:

- to be literally controlled by the love of Christ as expressed on the cross in the ultimate act of selflessness and sacrifice,
- to begin to see others as people for whom Christ died,
- to come to terms with the Lordship of Christ in our own lives,
- to begin to celebrate the fact that we are new creations of God and live up to that reputation,
- to embark upon a life where we are ambassadors for the Kingdom of God,
- to engage in the ministry of reconciliation,
- to create a unity mindset with others in place of always competing and performing for attention, and
- to begin to be open with others and modeling honesty and trust.

The quality of our message and the effectiveness it has in others is dependent upon our own spiritual world view and our spiritual health. We can pretend we have it all together, yet in the deeper levels of our living "hard drives" lies a greater truth, that truth being that we have not really been transformed by the truth but are only giving mental and verbal assent to it.

Christianity demands a divine confrontation with Christ to the point where our innermost being is filled with His

Spirit, a healing from misconceptions of the Christian life occurs. Only then can we communicate from personal experience, as truth — not some religious experience or concept — is the controlling force of our lives.

The unity we show, along with the purity of relationship that builds up and affirms, is the calling card of the church.

CHAPTER THREE

Why Bother? A Divine Set Up

While spending time in Eastern Europe, I met an elderly man who was very indoctrinated with the old school way of doing things and believing things. Since the collapse of the Iron Curtain, he had seen his life, and the lives of millions like his, fall into disarray and confusion. There was no government, no money, no security and no future hope.

Our initial encounter was not a pleasant one. Eno first tried to get rid of me, and then accused me of being a Western mercenary profiteering by using religion as tool for selfish gain. His contempt for religion was palatable. As we continued to communicate, however awkwardly via a translator, it was obvious that the translator was very uncomfortable and wanted this to end, and end immediately!

However, I felt an unusual compassion for this individual, and I persevered in our conversation. I discovered that he had lost his government pension as a result of the collapse of Communism, and that he now was seeing his family work longer and harder to earn even less. He had to come out of retirement and take a dead-end job just to help out. Eventually, he invited us to his workplace. He was a security guard at a half-constructed building; there was no hope of ever seeing the building being completed. It was a government project scuttled as a result of the changes.

After our day of ministry, supper and team de-briefing, my translator and I went to visit Eno. We entered a concrete building with building supplies stock-piled, open electrical wires, and puddles of water everywhere. Through 12-hour shifts, for weeks at a time, Eno made his home down in the basement in a nondescript room, with a small light, some books and a sheet of plywood for a bed. His job was to make sure nothing was stolen from the building, despite the fact that there would never be any plans to continue construction in the future.

I handed him a package of cookies, a gift in the customary tradition of Eastern Europeans. We sat wordless for long periods of time. From time to time Eno would ask skeptical questions as to my motives for being in his country. He found it hard to believe that someone would go through the expense of traveling all the way from my home to his, just to share Christ, and for no other reason.

After several hours we left to grab a couple of hours of sleep before we went out to minister throughout the day with the rest of the team. This happened for several nights, until the end of our ministry in the town. On Sunday morning, as we were preparing to leave for the next place of ministry, never to return to this town, the translator notified me that Eno wanted to see me one last time. This time, we were invited to his home, with his family. I went, not knowing what to expect. We were seated in the living room and through the translator; Eno told me that he had been thinking long and hard about what I had been telling him about Jesus, and that he had been reading the material in his own language we had given him. He went on to tell me he understood the material and what I had said to him, and after serious consideration, he was now ready, along with his family, to accept Jesus into his heart. We cried and prayed together and reluctantly parted — friends, brothers in Christ, and anticipating that we will share each other's friendship in eternity.

> Why bother? Because there are millions of Enos out there, desperately needing to hear and be transformed by the message of Jesus Christ.

Whenever I ask myself "why bother," this memory is one of several that springs up in my mind and heart. Eno had never met a westerner before; he believed what he had been told by his government; he understood that religion was mythological and for the weak. Now he is a child of the King! Keith Green used to challenge those at his concerts, saying that we shouldn't pray whether we should go to the mission field but whether God wants us to stay. Oswald Smith asked us whether anyone has the right to hear the Gospel twice when half of the world has not had the opportunity to hear it for the first time.

Why bother? Because there are millions of Enos out there, desperately needing to hear and be transformed by the message of Jesus Christ.

God rules and reigns!

The word "theology" means "the study of God." One of the most important bits of theological understanding a believer can have is an awareness of God's sovereignty.

The American Heritage Dictionary of the English Language defines sovereignty as, "supremacy of authority or rule as exercised by a sovereign or sovereign state ... complete independence and self-government ... a territory existing as an independent state." And the Eastman's Bible Dictionary defines sovereignty as God's "...absolute right to do all things according to His own good pleasure." Another definition is, "the quality or state of being sovereign, or of being a sovereign. The exercise of, or right to exercise, supreme power, dominion, sway, supremacy...."

From these definitions, you can see that when we are thinking or talking about God, we are thinking and talking about One who is the complete owner and ruler of all. This is much the same as the concept of Lordship, which we looked at in an earlier chapter.

With this in mind, we arrive at one of the world view "whys" — one of the reasons that explain why we need to have a world view that is in line with God's world view.

God is a "World View God," who always has His creation in mind. He transcends all cultures, barriers, languages, and differences and desires to communicate, through us, His amazing love for all.

Simply put, the sovereignty of God has been continually expressed over time and history. One commentator has said that history is literally "His-Story." Life, history, and all that is can only be understood when we begin to recognize the activity of God in daily life — past, present, and future.

We have been created in God's image to do God's work and reflect His glory here on earth. As a matter of fact, Peter says that we are a royal priesthood, a chosen generation, special people called out to reflect God's glory. Peter says that once we were "no people" before we accepted Christ as Saviour, but now we are "God's people". Each believer is someone, belonging to Someone, commissioned to let others know that they too can belong!

The concept of God as sovereign can be intimidating to some, and is simply rejected by others. In reality, once properly understood and embraced, this concept should bring joy and comfort to you. The reason for this is, our sovereign God is a loving God who looks out for us, directs the affairs of our lives, makes adjustments in us so that we can approach life with the proper attitude, and is always looking out for our success.

> God is a "World View God," who always has His creation in mind. He transcends all cultures, barriers, languages, and differences and desires to communicate, through us, His amazing love for all.

Ever feel like a loser? Well, God intends to change that! He is out to make you and me successful, by initiating in ours lives a new relationship with Him through Jesus Christ and joining us to a family that is loving, forgiving, friendly, and faithful. To have issues with the sovereignty of God is to have issues with authority and to harbor a rebellious attitude. A reluctance to embrace this truth has led to much misunderstanding. Many believers are walking around uncertain of their salvation, feeling like God is about to punish them for some unknown sin they have committed, fearful of a God whose motive is to make us miserable beggars. The Bible teaches the exact opposite! God loves us, has saved us, forgiven us, and desires above all things to restore in us principles that create success in our lives. That success begins with a clear conscience, a sense of forgiveness, a fresh, positive relationship with God, and a clear purpose in serving Him.

In the Old Testament book of Jeremiah, we find a prophecy pointing to what it will be like when we are redeemed by God through Jesus Christ. In chapter 31, three things are listed.

The first is that we will have a new heart motivated to serve Jesus, a heart that will beat after Him.

The second is that we will have a new teacher. John the apostle tells us that we have received the anointing, that we have the indwelling Holy Spirit who Jesus calls our Comforter and Counselor; this is the Holy Spirit who will teach us all things. What John is saying and what the Bible is teaching us is that now we have an intimate personal relationship with Jesus through the indwelling Holy Spirit, who is our guide through life.

…it is important that we completely understand that something of significance can actually be done to change people's lives for the better.

This leads to the third thing that is new in our lives according to Jeremiah 31. Jeremiah says, "no one will go to and fro saying 'know the Lord' for all shall know me". We as believers have a new relationship! All through the life of Jesus we see Jesus teaching and demonstrating that the His purpose in coming was to re-establish relationship with His lost creation. The result of this re-connection is that we will have a new heart that beats after God, a new teacher who instructs us in the way we should go, and new relationship that creates intimacy and understanding. In other words what was lost in the Fall of man is regained in the saving of man by Jesus.

When Jesus was crucified, one of the dramatic events that

took place was that the thick veil hung between the Holy Place and the Holy of Holies in the Temple was torn in two, from top to bottom! What this symbolized was that the death of Jesus was creating a way whereby each and every individual could enter His presence without punishment and death. Before this, only the High Priest could enter into the Holy of Holies, and only once a year. He would then come out with blood of bulls that was made holy and sprinkle it over the people on the Day of Atonement. Atonement means "to cover over" or "cover up". The priests' annual ceremony represented what Jesus would do permanently one day when the blood of bulls would be replaced with the blood of Jesus. With the atonement of Jesus, an annual symbol was unnecessary; Jesus' sacrifice guaranteed our permanent salvation.

What does this all have to do with missions, world view, and communicating cross-culturally? In order for us to have complete confidence in what we are doing, and for us to have a driving passion for the lost, it is important that we completely understand that something of significance can actually be done to change people's lives for the better.

> …we are called to be individuals participating in the Action of God over time and history…

It is equally important for us to know that God cares and that God has a plan that is far greater that our own good ideas about helping people out. Mother Teresa always kept in mind that all children are God's children, and so she could persevere until her dying day, no matter what obstacles she encountered and no matter how difficult the challenge she faced in Calcutta, India.

R.A. Tory, the early American evangelist, would simply proclaim, "Nothing but souls!" as he expressed what he was all about.

Reinard Bonke says that all he desires to do is "plunder Hell and populate Heaven." All these people and countless others, in differing ways, are expressing a purpose that is greater than themselves. This is the answer to the bigger question as to why Christians evangelize and involve themselves in missions. Because there is a greater mission than just one person being involved in an activity; we are called to be individuals participating in the Action of God over time and history ... and that is your calling, too!

God's end-time plan:

Paul declares that Jesus Christ was "slain before the foundations of the world". However difficult it may be to understand this truth, it is evident that in the heart and mind of God, the death of Jesus was no after-thought or impulsive reaction to a human tragedy. There was a clearly thought out, divine agenda through which God expresses His love for humanity and through which He will deal with the impending sin problem in which humans would find themselves trapped.

When, as believers, we find ourselves involved in ministry of any kind, whether it be full time church work or market place work where we are influencing and sharing our faith, we are involving ourselves in God's agenda of reaching people who He loves and for whom He died on the cross. God's agenda is to bring unto Himself a people who He calls the church, to discover their rightful place of intimacy with Him and fulfillment through Him.

The chain of events is clear! Jesus comes and dies on the cross, leaving twelve disciples who become the apostles of the Church, and 120 believers in an upper room somewhere in Jerusalem to pray.

Why Bother? A Divine Set Up

In the book of Acts we find that an amazing phenomenon occurs as the Holy Spirit falls upon all who were there and they begin to speak in other tongues or languages and move out into the packed streets of the city where a national religious festival was taking place. Those who were listening to the believers heard, in their own languages, praises being given to God as well as uplifting messages from those who had never known how to speak their language before.

> ...this rapidly-spreading Christian church brings about changed societies and countries.

They also witnessed a group of people, who were known to be fearful and withdrawn, now completely changed. These formerly timid folk began to boldly and unashamedly proclaim their faith in Jesus Christ. Peter, who mere days ago had denied even knowing Jesus at His arrest, now stands up in front of a massive crowd and shares the Gospel of the Good News. The result was that over 3,000 people made decisions for Christ that day and were baptized in water. Peter's words are clear and powerful. He quotes scripture verses from the Old Testament, showing that the visitation of the Holy Spirit in the "upper room" was a fulfillment of what the Jewish people had been waiting for for thousands of years, as foretold by their prophets.

A few days later, another huge crowd hears the Gospel and over 5,000 more make decisions for Jesus. In the following days, the new church begins to take shape and they continue to follow the schedule of the Jewish schedule of Sabbath and special ceremonies, and also begin to meet in individuals' homes throughout the week. They create a communal society of their own, sharing everything they had with others who were needy or less fortunate. The apostles as well as other gifted believers continue to preach and teach the Gospel in Jerusalem and other parts of Israel.

> Zwingli would use this story to make the point that Jesus' intention was for us to continue to carry the cause of Christ; that we are God's plan for the end of the ages.

The new believers, who are primarily converted Jews, begin to feel the heat from the religious leaders; a persecution breaks out. They are driven from their homes, work places, and religious institutions. They take flight to other parts of the populated world. As they find safe havens, they settle down and begin to build new lives for themselves. As they do so, they meet together to encourage each other, pray, read scriptures, and share their faith with others in the villages, towns, and cities they are now in. There is literally a multiplication of believers in the church, which soon includes people of all tribes, tongues, and creeds. Eventually, this rapidly-spreading Christian church brings about changed societies and countries.

For two thousand years this process has been happening in one way or another, to one degree or another, in one place or another. Sometimes the Christian church has failed miserably; at times it has been persecuted mercilessly; and at times it has triumphed gloriously. But no matter how it looks from the outside, Jesus made a promise that will, in the end, come to full realization. He said He would, "build my church and the gates of hell would not prevail against it!" You and I are part of this grand scheme and when we involve ourselves in the Great Commission, we are joining the ranks of the millions who have gone on before and the millions who are involved at present to spread the Good News that Jesus died so that we don't have to; we can live eternally.

No back-up plans!

There is a story about Ulrich Zwingli, one of the leaders of the Protestant Reformation. Zwingli was a Swiss minister who aligned himself with Martin Luther, the Father of the Reformation. Luther's greatest teaching was that it was by grace we are saved, not of works, and that all believers were priests unto God. The Reformers re-discovered these and many other good, biblical teachings that had largely been ignored for hundreds of years.

Zwingli, however, was more militant about his beliefs and was involved in more radical efforts to make his point. He told a story set just after the point when Jesus died and rose from the dead. In Zwingli's story, when Jesus ascended into heaven, He met up with many of the Old Testament leaders and prophets who were ecstatic and began to provide positive feedback to Jesus about how brilliant the scheme was to destroy the works of the devil, and how He had so successfully died on behalf of His creation, setting them free from sin and death.

At one point in the meeting, someone asked what His next move was going to be. Jesus told them He had 120 believers who were going to share the Gospel and that from there, a world Christian movement would begin that would multiply out and continue until the Father said it was time to return for His bride, the church. Zwingli said that the patriarchs were aghast at this comment, and began to protest, saying that humans were weak and uncommitted. They went on to say how that plan was lousy and would end up failing because people would fail Him. So they began to question Jesus about His back-up plans, should that plan fail.

Jesus' response was that He had no other plan. This was the only plan. Zwingli would use this story to make the point that Jesus' intention was for us to continue to carry the cause of Christ; that we are God's plan for the end of the ages. And that we are to take seriously and with commitment the call to reach the lost in our generation.

In the Gospel of Luke, chapter 24, we find an amazing portion of scripture that not only includes the Great Commission but also the events that lead up to the commissioning of the church by Jesus. In it is a simple but powerful revelation of what has been provided to the missionary from God.

Luke 24:36-53:

While they were saying these things, Jesus Himself stood among them and said to them, "Peace be with you." But they were startled and terrified, thinking they saw a ghost. Then He said to them, "Why are you frightened, and why do doubts arise in your hearts? Look at my hands and my feet; it's me! Touch me and see; a ghost does not have flesh and bones like you see I have." When He had said this, He showed them His hands and His feet. And while they still could not believe it (because of their joy) and were amazed, He said to them, "Do you have anything here to eat?" So they gave Him a piece of broiled fish, and He took it and ate it in front of them. Then He said to them, "These are my words that I spoke to you while I was still with you, that everything written about me in the law of Moses and the prophets and the psalms must be fulfilled." Then He opened their minds so they could understand the scriptures, and said to them, "Thus it stands written that the Messiah would suffer and would rise from the dead on the third day, and repentance for the forgiveness of sins would be proclaimed in His name to all nations, beginning from Jerusalem. You are witnesses of these things. And look, I am sending you what my Father promised. But stay in the city until you have been clothed with power from on high." Then Jesus led them out as far as Bethany, and lifting up His hands, He blessed them. Now during the blessing He departed and was taken up into heaven. So they worshiped Him and returned to Jerusalem with great joy, and were continually in the temple courts blessing God.

The authority of our message:

It begins with the opening scene where the disciples are huddled in a room after the arrest, trial, crucifixion, and burial of Jesus. They have locked themselves in this room, fearing that they would be the next victims of the Roman government and would be crucified along with Jesus. They are feeling abandoned, alone, and in serious trouble. Some are angry, some are discouraged, some are making plans to begin to take up the regular routine of lives they once knew as fishermen, tax collectors, or in the other trades they once practiced. Some have given up hope as to who Jesus is, and are in complete disbelief.

...no matter where we are in the world, one of the most outstanding elements of power we have is the authority of the resurrection.

Then, from out of nowhere, without the using door or window, Jesus appears! They honestly believe that they are seeing a ghost or some other kind of apparition. They are fearful and dazed. Then Jesus begins to speak to them and questions why they are doubtful. Thomas says he will not believe unless he sees the nail prints in Jesus' hands and the hole in His side, where the Roman centurion's spear had been thrust into it.

Jesus gestures to Thomas, inviting him to place his fingers in the holes in His hands and to place his hand in the hole in His side. After questioning the disciples as to why they were frightened, and showing His hands and feet, He emphasizes that He is not a ghost. He invites them to allay their fears by touching Him. Now their fear turns into joy, and Jesus asks for a piece of broiled fish and eats it in front of them.

Was this just a nice story, or was Jesus just trying to make some kind of re-connection with them? No, as a matter of fact, what we have unfolding before our eyes is Jesus demonstrating to the disciples (and through them to the whole world!) that He physically was raised from the dead. Christianity stands or falls on this one central truth — whether the resurrection actually happened, and if so, was it a physical resurrection or some kind of spiritual one?

Developing a Christian world view not only rests upon the fact of the resurrection of Jesus Christ as God but also on the power of the Word of God.

Paul the apostle, a very intelligent man, had absolutely no doubt as to the real, physical resurrection of Christ. Paul states in 2 Corinthians that if Christ is not raised from the dead then we who call ourselves Christians are most to be pitied! He goes on to say that we might as well join the rest of the world and begin to eat, drink, and be merry for tomorrow we will die too. In other words if all there is to live for is this world, and there is no hope after the grave, let's party until we drop! But in this same chapter of 2 Corinthians, Paul goes on to write an eloquent argument about how Christ indeed has been raised and that we therefore need to adjust our compasses for our lives in accordance with that truth.

The physical resurrection of Jesus first of all fulfills all the Old Testament prophesies (read Isaiah 53). Secondly, it provides the support for the argument of who Christ is as Messiah and God. Thirdly, it offers every person ever born, hope beyond the grave. When it comes to developing a Christian world view, it also brings the assurance we need to boldly proclaim the Gospel and all its teachings as truth. When we are in the trenches of sharing our faith, no matter where we are in the world, one of the most outstanding elements of power we have is the authority of the resurrection.

Meanwhile, back in that room in Jerusalem — as the discussion unfolds, Jesus (over a piece of broiled fish) begins to make a statement. He tells the disciples that what has happened in His life, including the physical resurrection, was exactly what He had told them while He was with them. He also says that it was all written about thousands of years before in the law of Moses, the prophets, and the psalms. In other words, the life of Jesus, the words of Jesus, the miracles He performed, and deeds He did were not some spontaneous afterthought. They were not the actions of some good person doing good things. This was the fulfillment of a plan hatched in eternity to free man from the clutches of Satan's power. As Jesus related these things, the Bible says He opened the disciples' minds to understand the scriptures in the Old Testament so that they could see that those scriptures all pointed to Him.

Remember, from the first chapter of this book, the story of the theological scholar who maintained that the most profound thing he had learned was "Jesus loves me this I know for the Bible tells me so"? In addition to his declaration of the importance of the love of Jesus, this scholar was also stating his faith in the written word of God. He was agreeing that the Bible, after all the critical analysis, after all the questions, after all the debating, after all the outright assaults, was still the most mesmerizing, most powerful book on the planet.

Developing a Christian world view not only rests upon the fact of the resurrection of Jesus Christ as God but also on the power of the Word of God.

The content of our message:

As the discussion unfolds, Jesus begins to synthesize the whole message into concise points. Jesus says, "... the Messiah would suffer and would rise from the dead on the third day, and repentance for the forgiveness of sins would be proclaimed in His name ..."

In developing a Christian world view, we have the content of the Gospel laid out before us by the Master Story Teller, Jesus Himself.

The church often gets bogged down in religious detail or ensnared in political issues. It often involves itself in things that become a distraction from its central purpose. Being involved in church life for some years, I understand the need for dealing with religious issues and taking on some political positions, but when it comes at the expense of the central message and task of the church, it becomes counterproductive for the Gospel and limiting to the needy.

Here, Jesus establishes a first priority message for the church that is to remain the standard for ever. It's one thing to "get" the Great Commission to go into all the world but it's another thing to "get" what we are to say. Today, with the overwhelming amount of material to learn from, and the pervasive technology that allows us to access information anytime, anywhere, it is easy to lose focus and get confused about exactly what it is we as Christians are to say.

Here Jesus brings us back to the basics. In many churches today, a declaration known as The Apostles' Creed is still sung or quoted. The content sums up the beliefs of Christians; it includes the truths in this verse.

At the end of the day Jesus served up for us a very powerful, simple, and effective message to share with the world. In developing a Christian world view, we have the content of the Gospel laid out before us by the Master Story Teller, Jesus Himself.

The tool of our message:

Studies today show that people are more willing to give to tangible projects or to people they are in relationship with, rather than to some generic corporate head office somewhere in another part of the country or the world. In response to this reality, projects, programs and strategies have been developed to assist in motivating people to commit financial resources to missions. Overall the plan seems to be working.

However, I am afraid of a severe backlash that will result in many good things being supported financially, but also in a lack of manpower to actually work the things into some useful goal. Recently, in a missions emphasis service, I was asked to introduce the second offering that would be going to generally support missionaries. As I spoke, I challenged the crowd about the importance of first recognizing that we can leverage our dollars by sending them to an organization that could recruit, train, administer, and oversee a missions ministry beyond what we could do. Second, I urged them to support approved, well-trained personnel to stay on the mission field.

As I spoke, I felt the distance of the crowd. It wasn't a sense of rebellion but more of a reaction to something many of them had not heard before, being recent Christians in a place where this concept had long since been dropped by the boards. From their understanding, they were the only ones who could accomplish what needed to be done, others could not be trusted, and that what I was suggested was good money being thrown after bad money. Needless to say the offering was anything but overwhelming.

In a disposable society like ours with a need to see a "good return" and something material to feel that our investment is worthwhile, we are beginning to lose the realization that the greatest force on the planet is still people. It's not technology, not machinery, not media. Jesus could have just as well openly prophesied that there would come a time when media, technology and whatever other clever invention of man would be sufficient to accomplish the task of world missions. He didn't! Jesus lays out for the disciples that they are to be witnesses of the things they had experienced, and that the church — the people of God, nothing else — is to be the force for the Gospel on earth.

The power of our message:

Jesus' last directive in this passage of Scripture was for the disciples to stay in the city until they were clothed with power from on high. What Jesus also said was that He was going to give them the Promise of the Father. As you study the Old Testament, you will find that one of the major teachings was a promise God gave the Jews. They looked for the promise to be fulfilled in the end times. That promise was based upon the covenants God gave; there were three primary elements to it. One was that the people of God would receive a blessing; another was that they would become a people; and the third was that they would be given a land to call their own. These promises were interpreted in many differing ways over the years during the Old Testament era and in the time between the Testaments. This created much confusion for the Jews concerning their expectations of what the Messiah would accomplish.

The piece that was missing in their understanding was that the Messiah — the Anointed One — would first come to die for their sin. Second, He would come back to set up a physical kingdom on a new earth and in a new heaven. But before any of this could take place, there was a need for Jesus to confront the evil forces that control His creation. He did this by dying on the cross, and setting humans free from sin.

What was anticipated in the Old Testament was a time when the Spirit of God would indwell humans and a "power" would be given to obey and serve God. This "power" is the Holy Spirit, who comes to enable us to serve God, have an intimate relationship with God, and become part of the family of God. All three aspects of God's promise were fulfilled by Jesus dying on the cross. We have a new relationship with God where once we had none because of sin, and we have the Holy Spirit residing in us to provide the ability to serve Him. So the power of our message as world view Christians is the indwelling Holy Spirit who convicts of sin when we go astray, who provides the ability to live a holy life, who opens the way to have a relationship with God, and who provides us with a heart to pass this message to others. Oswald Smith, a missionary statesman, once said, "Every heart without Christ is a mission field and every heart with Christ is a missionary".

> Jesus lays out for the disciples that they are to be witnesses of the things they had experienced, and that the church — the people of God, nothing else — is to be the force for the Gospel on earth.

Summary:

In attempting to answer the question, why bother becoming a Christian with a world view, it is easy to see that we bother because as believers we are called to be involved in something greater than ourselves or anything temporal here on earth. We are joining up to be a part of God's sovereign purpose and plan. We are also provided with an opportunity to get involved in God's plan of salvation for the whole world. This means to be in a wonderful situation where we pass on to others what has been passed to us, and that we join the purpose of the church in sharing the message of Jesus Christ. This includes having the authority, content, tool, and power of the Great Commission working in our lives.

As we carry this world view in life, we are synchronizing with God's timing in our lives and the world. We are also reflecting our gratitude and thanksgiving for what He has done in the world, on the cross, and in our lives. By bothering to be involved in the world as Christians, we are doing the "works" of the Father as Jesus did and called us to, reflecting His love and grace, demonstrating His foreknowledge in that we are sharing a historical act that was planed ahead of all time for others, and delivering a special message of revelation to others.

I once heard a story about a criminal going to the hanging gallows in England during the time there were public executions. As the sentenced person would walk up to the place of hanging, a minister would follow him or her and read scripture and make statements about the importance of repenting before dying and going to hell. All the dark and fearful statements about Hell would be recited.

This particular criminal is said to have turned and asked if the minister truly believed what he was reading aloud and saying. Before the minister ever had an opportunity to respond, the criminal said, "Because if I did I would crawl barefooted on broken glass across this country to share it!" This criminal saw something that was more important than life. It was that, if there is a truth that points to the existence of an eternity and there is a heaven to gain and a hell to lose, then there is a purpose to life and there is a reason to be active in the spreading of the message.

CHAPTER FOUR

Components of Cross-Cultural Communication

During the 1976 Montreal Olympics, I had the opportunity to participate in my very first evangelistic outreach. It was organized by Youth With A Mission, and Lorne Cunningham was leading the way and taking part in some of the training. For me, as a new believer, it was all very exciting; I was like a dry sponge wanting to soak in everything there was to absorb. In one particular session, Lorne challenged the team to "go barefoot." He told us about the concept of a "bond slave," as portrayed in the Bible. Essentially, a bond slave is a person who voluntarily chooses to commit themselves to their owner as a slave for life. This was marked by a ceremony, as the bondslave gave a shoe or sandal to the master. The owner would then accept the slave, bore a hole in his or her ear and place a ring in it, signifying that the person belonged to the master for life.

When this was done, three things were true of such a slave. One — they had no say in the matter of where they were coming from. Two — they had no say in where they were headed. Three — they had nothing to say about what was happening to them in the present. All the slave had was a trust in the master, that he would properly take care of him or her as cherished property, protect him or her from the abuse of others, and ensure the slave's goodwill.

In this chapter, we will look at the aspects of cross cultural communication, and consider the character of God, whom we are to communicate. As we walk down this road, the posture that will never lead us astray in our attempt to be excellent in serving others is the one of slave. So, as we read on, let's "go barefoot!"

Culture:

We have looked at the motives for developing a Christian world view, a biblical model for developing a Christian world view, and why we as Christians should anchor our thoughts and actions in a Christian world view. Hopefully, we have clearly directed our thinking toward the proper attitude, the biblical rationale, and the perspective we need to approach reaching the lost for Christ.

One more point should be made in order to underscore the importance of this mission. In chapter four of the Gospel of Luke there is a fascinating story. We meet Jesus coming out from His forty days of fasting in the wilderness; He enters a synagogue to preach.

"Then He rolled up the scroll, gave it back to the attendant, and sat down. The eyes of everyone in the synagogue were fixed on Him. Then He began to tell them, 'Today this scripture has been fulfilled even as you heard it being read.' All were speaking well of Him, and were amazed at the gracious words coming out of His mouth. They said, 'Isn't this Joseph's son?' Jesus said to them, 'No doubt you will quote to me the proverb, "Physician, heal yourself!" and say, "What we have heard that you did in Capernaum, do here in your hometown too." And He added, 'I tell you the truth, no prophet is acceptable in his hometown. But in truth I tell you, there were many widows in Israel in Elijah's days, when the sky was shut up three and a half years, and there was a great famine over all the land. Yet Elijah was sent to none of them, but only to a woman who was a widow at Zarephath in Sidon. And there were many lepers in Israel in the time of the prophet Elisha, yet none of them was cleansed except Naaman the Syrian.' "

Jesus is asked to read the Scripture for that day and the appointed passage is from the book of Isaiah. So Jesus reads the powerful words of the prophet, declaring that the Spirit of Lord is upon Him to preach, heal, open eyes of the blind, and set the captive free. He then begins to give His message. At the end of His time of sharing the people are astounded by His wisdom, brilliance, and authority with which He speaks. Jesus then goes on to to refer to a couple of stories from the Old Testament where God performed miracles. One concerned the widow Zarephath who lived in Sidon and was miraculously fed, and the other was about Naaman the Syrian, who was healed from leprosy.

These stories enraged those who were listening to Him and in a matter of minutes Jesus goes from hero to heal! They swarm Him, take Him out to the edge of a cliff and attempt to kill Him by throwing Him down. Imagine a crowd of people who were fawning over Him and saying fantastic things about His preaching and His eloquence all of a sudden taking issue with a couple of stories He tells from their very own Scripture.

What was it that was so devastating as to make a group of good synagogue-going people turn into a lynch mob? When you explore the passages of Scripture Jesus used, you will notice that both of the miracles took place in the lives of people who were not Jews but pagans ... unbelievers. The Jews, especially the leaders of Jesus' day, had a very nationalistic concept of God; they understood that all the promises, all the blessings, and all the attention was to be on them and that any form of judgment from God would be upon those outside the Jewish belief. They had been waiting for a Messiah to come and destroy all other people and set up a kingdom that would be theirs, exclusively.

Jesus, at the outset of His public ministry on earth, was making the point that His message and His love were intended for the whole world; none were to be left out. We see this message illustrated over and over again in His ministry. The woman at the well in John chapter three was first of all, a woman! She was also a Samaritan who was to be avoided at all costs (the land of Samaria was to be passed by without even being stepped on); and most of all she was an adulteress. Jesus also tells the disciples that He has sheep who are not of "this fold," implying that His message was universal.

We see that God is a missionary God who sent His Son for the whole world, as John the Apostle says in chapter three, verse sixteen. So now we turn our attention to the practical components of what it means to have a Christian world view. As a starting point we will choose Carley Dodd's definition of culture: "The total accumulation of an identifiable group's beliefs, norms, activities, institutions, and communication patterns."

"Beliefs" comprise the common understanding of the world view of a group of people. "Activities" are the routines that are involved within any given culture. "Institutions" are the social priorities engaged in by the culture. And "communication patterns" are the verbal and non-verbal ways utilized to create understanding between individuals in a particular culture.

The list Dodd presents includes all the elements involved in sending or receiving meaningful communication to and from anyone else on the planet. Cultural differences are those elements which either create and environment of comfort or create and environment of tension or even a breeding ground for outright hate for others. Remember this definition because it has an impact on who you are, and how you approach others.

> Jesus, at the outset of His public ministry on earth, was making the point that His message and His love were intended for the whole world; none were to be left out.

Because we grow and develop as human beings, mainly through the influence of our society, family, communities, and schools, we tend to create our world view, or window, of how we perceive and understand the world around us, fairly unconsciously. This means that we do not readily or easily understand we communicate or filter the communication of others.

None the less, although we may not recognize the process of filtering communications and perceptions through our world view, that process is very real. The automatic processing of communication through our existing filters is inherent in who we are. It is also necessary — if we had to interpret from scratch every little aspect of communication, we wouldn't even get out of bed in the morning! It would just be too overwhelming and confusing.

So we create assumptions and categories, we put everything into nice little boxes so we can cope. However, when differences occur due to meeting different people with different views on life, people who are coming from (and filtering through) an entirely different culture, as defined by Dodd, tension is created and emotions are engaged, resulting in all kinds of reactions in us. Even the slightest differences can become serious barriers to communication. For example, consider differences in attitudes toward:

• Time. Have you ever been frustrated by people who do not respect your time? Have you ever been frustrated at people who are so uptight at punctuality?

• Property. Did you ever have a disagreement over the understanding of ownership of something — such as a fight with a sibling over clothes? Have you ever wondered how racist phrases such as "Indian giver" came about? When the first settlers came to North America and established relationships with Indians there were, to say the least, some cultural issues. One of them concerned the understanding of the idea of "property". The native North Americans, in a hospitable gesture toward the settlers, would sometimes "give" blankets to keep them warm; or similarly offer other kinds of objects. The settlers were ecstatic about this, until the native people wanted their property back. The settlers couldn't understand what was happening. In Europe, culturally, when something was "given," it was for keeps. The Native North Americans' cultural understanding of providing help such as this was a gift for the time it was needed, with the expectation of ultimately receiving the objects back! Wars have been created over matters even more insignificant that this.

• Dress. Have you ever been the victim of fashion bigotry? Have you ever instantly associated someone's dress with loose morality? With generational incompatibility? With spiritual astuteness or a lack thereof? My wife was once accused of wearing "hooker boots," at Bible College! Don't laugh — she also was told that not wearing nylons would lead to pregnancy! Okay, maybe we should laugh.

• Food. Within the culture of North American churches, there has always been a controversy between those who approve of casual or social drinking and those who hold a position of total abstinence from the consumption of alcoholic beverages. That controversy has never been solved, even though everyone involved is speaking the same cultural language! Imagine how, in culturally divers places, many such issues can be the difference between effective relating and communicating and total disaster.

• Personal Space. Have you ever been accused of being in someone's face too much? Or maybe of being too "standoffish"? Individuals have a cultural barrier as to how far or how close someone should be in order to create a comfort in communication. Whole societies also have this "bubble" which indicates many things, from sincerity to affection to communication.

• Beauty. One of my sons told me of a special on the Learning Channel that recounted what was "pleasing" to a man in relation to various aspects of women. Some cultures, for example, seemed to have a foot fetish, others prefer a certain weight, and others ... well, I think you can grasp the illustration. At any rate I, as a father, was quick to assure him that when it comes to the male species that any or all aspects were an issue — which of course he was only too happy to agree with.

• Entertainment. How one engages in social activities also creates a sense of affinity or disconnect within cultures or in between differing cultures.

• Work. In an interview I did just after the Iron Curtain fell in the Soviet Union, I was asked about the differing cultures of the East and West. This question came at the end of a rather long meeting where many were tired from the sheer volume of discussion between Westerners and Easterners, a discussion that had been long overdue ... by at least 70 years! At any rate, one of the interpreters with me decided to jump in and summarize what could have been a long answer. His reply was that in the West, when you get up and it's a nice day you have to go to work, while in the East, if the same happens, you don't go to work but you get paid, anyway.

Work is an historical and cultural understanding. There are books on the market today that deal with hard work, smart work, the end of work, the knowledge worker, etc. When we lay our cultural attitude toward work over onto other cultures, we may create a frustration

> The goal is to be aware, first, of the existence of these differences; second, to attempt to identify and understand these differences; and third, to prepare a strategy to cope with them.

- Values. A cross-cultural specialist once taught a class for a short term missions team. His topic was "Cultural Sins;" he made the point that when we travel outside our cultural context, emphasis on some values, even within Christianity, can cause clashes. It was eye opening and somewhat stunning to those unaware of any kind of cultural differences. Our values can be a hindrance to our communicating cross-culturally, and in developing a Christian world view.

- Competition. Our rugged individualism and competitive nature can also become a challenging trait when communicating cross-culturally. Other cultures may approach achievement in differing ways that do not necessarily employ competition as we know it. So to go into a different culture with the "me first," "gotta win" philosophy can be perceived in a negative way, not as the positive attribute that we North Americans may tend to assume.

Other aspects of cultural differences include inherent concepts of what is fair, ethical, or considered to be a value. One very important thing to note here is that all cultures have developed unique prescriptions for living, but that these unique features of the culture may not be readily apparent. They may not even be well understood by people who have simply assimilated these cultural features subconsciously. However, these differences can lead to devastating outcomes if those attempting a cross-cultural experience fail to assume that such features exist. The goal is to be aware, first, of the existence of these differences; second, to attempt to identify and understand these differences; and third, to prepare a strategy to cope with them. Our personality orientation can either assist in creating success in this area or can limit our effectiveness. An empathetic person has an enormous head start in this area.

As long as this list of potential cultural stumbling blocks is, there are literally hundreds of other issues that become insurmountable walls to communication and effective relationship building. The key is to begin to become aware of our own cultural features, to learn to identify them and to understand them. Because we, of course, have as many such issues as anyone coming from any other cultural world view. Only when we are aware of our own cultural idiosyncrasies, can we proceed, in turn, to create a sensitivity and insight to others' cultures. That, in turn, becomes our starting point on which we can build bridges of communication.

Culture comes from learned rules about proper behavior and unconscious pre-conditions that serve to help us cope and understand the world we live in. Culture is literally the glue that bonds us to other people and creates an identity for us so that we can have a sense of safety, community and comfort. When this sense of safety and comfort is threatened, we are being culturally challenged. This may occur within our own culture, through generational differences or geographical differences.

We constantly carry culture around with us like luggage; every day we take out survival tools, information, references, associations, and personal goals that meet our daily life needs. From our cultural understanding — which more often is unconscious than conscious — we apply rituals and rules that create understanding and commonality between us and others. Simple examples can include the hand shake, or a verbal greeting of, "Hi. How are you?" These are very basic but essential parts of culture that indicate friendship, acceptance, and acknowledgement of another person. Without mutually understood cultural acts such as these, uncertainty can be generated in others, leading to insecurity or a sense of offense or rejection.

Only when we are aware of our own cultural idiosyncrasies, can we proceed, in turn, to create a sensitivity and insight to others' cultures.
That, in turn, becomes our starting point on which we can build bridges of communication.

This may sound like overkill, but I assure you that if you take conscious note of it the next time, you will see it works. For instance, guys, greet your male buddy with kisses on each cheek the next time you see him in place of a handshake or pat on the back, and note the reaction. You may hear words like "Weird," or "strange," — or worse; you may see a look of shock or surprise; you may even see physical backing off. What you are experiencing is a cultural disconnect or dissonance, because your friend has no reference point or understanding of what is going on.

North Americans, who tend to be casual about greetings, can often encounter "hand-shake" misunderstandings in parts of Europe, where greeting with a handshake is a very significant part of any meeting between friends or acquaintances.

Just saying "hello" and not shaking hands will probably be interpreted as an insult.

Social identity

Let's consider the centerpiece of a Christian's culture and the development of a world view. As God's creations, we are by nature designed for relationship and interaction. We are, simply stated, social beings! The blessing of redemption and being part of the Christian life is that we have been reconnected relationally with our Creator as well as with each other.

The New Testament is full of admonitions to love one another, to be at peace with one another, to serve one another, and to forgive one another. Our identity, salvation and health are all reflected in our sense of community. Paul the apostle speaks about this when he tells us we were "no people" but now we are "God's people." He also talks about how we once were estranged from the "commonwealth" (which means "community") but now we are part of it. These, as well as many other teachings in the Bible, speak of the importance, the need, and the necessity of living in relationship together as Christians.

Sociologists and anthropologists all point to the human need to have some kind of affiliation with someone or some group in order to have a sense of well-being. Where they speak of "affiliation," the Bible speaks of "relationship." The Fall of Adam and Eve brought the most severe consequence ever inflicted upon human beings. That consequence was a broken relationship with God the Father.

The idea of God being our Father today can bring up some very different pictures in our minds — some good, some not so good. Taken from a human point of view, filtered through negative experiences some of us may have had, the image of "Father" may be one of a dictator, abuser, rejecter, or something totally undefined. But from the Bible's perspective, the idea of "Father" is meant to represent One who will fill every need, One whose relationship we have been missing ever since Adam sinned. Jesus redefined "Father" for the people of His day, when He challenged them to call God "Abba" — meaning "Daddy." He intended us to see God, not through the lens of our pain and experience, but through the lens of our inherent understand of what "Father" is supposed to be.

When Jesus came, He revealed who the Father was. In essence, He revealed to us that God is intricately part of His creation, and very interested it having a relationship with it.

God is our Father

In the Sermon on the Mount, Jesus chose a most unusual word for God. "Let your light shine before men in such a way that they may see your good works, and glorify your Father who is in heaven." Here, Jesus referred to God as "Father". This was a major change from the understanding of God as being totally different and far off. The use of "Father" implied tenderness in place of a sternness. It also implied closeness, instead of a distance that could not be overcome. When Jesus came, He revealed who the Father was. In essence, He revealed to us that God is intricately part of His creation, and very interested it having a relationship with it.

The Father loves the Son

"The Father loves the Son, and has given all things into His hand." (John 3:35)

"For the Father loves the Son, and shows Him all things that He Himself is doing; and greater works than these will He show Him, that you may marvel." (John 5:20)

"Just as the Father has loved Me, I have also loved you; abide in My love." (John 15:9)

Jesus came to reflect the Father, to provide for us an opportunity to see into His nature, and to model what that relationship could look like. The word "abiding" means a continual interacting with or constant presence. Jesus calls us to stay close, enjoy, trust, and allow the Father to reveal to us the greatest event on the planet ... Himself.

The Father is in heaven

"Thy kingdom come, Thy will be done, on earth as it is in heaven." In the Lord's Prayer, Jesus reveals that God's desire is for us to experience, here and right now, the reality of a great relationship with Him. Jesus opened the door of opportunity so we can relate to, enjoy, and have affinity with God the Creator.

The Father has life in Himself

At Creation, God breathed life into us. His breath validates us as significant; His breath gives life to the body; and His breath quickens and energizes the human spirit. When each of us followed Adam's path into sin, it was as though our source of breath was cut off. The psychological challenges, emotional distortions, physical lethargy, and spiritual voids we experience within ourselves all have their root problem in attempting to live life apart from the life God provides for us in relationship with Him. Abiding in God is the life line we need to sustain and move through this uncertain, volatile world. For the believer, we have a Father to support us, protect us, direct us, and care for us.

The Father gives life

God not only has life in Himself, but His character is to give it away to those who come to Him.

The Father knows best

Jesus told His disciples that He did whatever the Father told Him to do. His dependence and trust were so intertwined with the Father that it was literally indistinguishable as to who was who! The relationship the Father offers us, allows us to have the same power and opportunity should we engage in it. "For all these things the Gentiles eagerly seek; for your heavenly Father knows that you need all these things." (Matthew 6:32)

The Father is always at work

Our Heavenly Father has one desire for us. He, by His Spirit, is constantly working to bring that desire into its full effect. His desire for us is that we be like Christ. Therefore, the goal of every believer should be, to be conformed into the image of Christ, literally to act, look, talk, and think like Jesus. To live in the understanding that He is always there.

Do you know the poem "Footprints," written by Margaret Fishback Powers? Briefly, it's about a person who believes in God; however, when she looks back on her life, she sees that sometimes, there are two sets of footprints in the sand of life, as she walks beside God. But other times, there was only one set of footprints in the sand of life. She concludes that those were the times when God left her alone. God's reply was that when there was only one set of footprints in the sand, those were the times when He carried that person.

It may not always look like we are on the winning side, or that God cares about us, but one thing is certain from God's perspective — for the believer, "it's all good". Paul declares in Romans that, "In all things He works for the good". Some have interpreted this to mean that all circumstances just happen to work out, no matter how evil or bad they are. I don't think that's what this means. Instead, I believe the accurate interpretation is, no matter what happens to a believer (even being a martyr), God is there working out the situation for our ultimate good.

In light of what this chapter is about — "Components of Cross-Cultural Communication" — you may ask what this has to do with the "price of eggs"! It has everything to do with it. For far too long the church has not understood the message it is to bring to its people, or to the people outside the church. As a consequence, we adopt slogans and statements that actually push people away from the church, as we attempt to ram down people's throats a religious concept of God and Christianity in place of the wonderful message Jesus intended us to hear, the truth He died to bring about. Who God is — as stated in the paragraphs above — is the essence of what we are to know, experience, and share with others who don't know God.

For far too long the church has not understood the message it is to bring to its people, or to the people outside the church. As a consequence, we adopt slogans and statements that actually push people away from the church,

---

The question is, are we on our way out the door to give a message we don't yet have a grasp on? A "ready, fire, aim" strategy will not work here! The quality must go in before the name goes on!

The need or desire for affinity or affiliation is not something new, and as a matter of fact, is a spiritual need more than a social one. It stems from an empty heart that the world cannot fill. The message of the Gospel, the message we bring to a world that is lost and dying, is Good News! People's hearts are empty; we know the One who will fill them. People long for relationship; we know the One who is the source of all good relationships. We have the answer to humanity's ultimate need — now, that is an opportunity to be taken advantage of!

When this truth is fully comprehended I actually believe that we never fully "get it," but that coming to understand the truth is a journey we embark upon. Our journey includes certain events through which we come to more and more realize this truth.

> ...if we are launched on mission prematurely with a "go get 'em boys" mind-set that leaves no room for real understanding or communication, we stand to lose everything we hope to accomplish.

Having said that, when this truth is comprehended, there will be major ramifications in our lives. "Affiliation," say sociologists, influences behavior and creates a perspective on what is right or wrong, what is appropriate or inappropriate. In other words, our sense of affiliation determines to a large degree what resonates within us as to values and world view.

At the crossroads of culture, or world view, lie the tensions, misconceptions, and challenges of mission work. It is the responsibility of the believer (in this case, the missionary) to take the initiative to share the message. However, if this is done with only a superficial cultural understanding, if we are launched on mission prematurely with a "go get 'em boys" mind-set that leaves no room for real understanding or communication, we stand to lose everything we hope to accomplish.

Not only does the Christian truth appeal to people's need for a sense of community or affiliation, but it also brings a clarity as to who God is. During the life and times of Jesus, there were many leaders walking around proclaiming themselves as the Messiah. There were also those who were, with great confidence, teaching false attributes and characteristics of what the Messiah would look like and mistaken descriptions of the events that would bring on the coming of the Messiah.

> The need in evangelism and missions is to relate to others a proper understanding of who God is and to believe and pray for the Holy Spirit to do the inner work of convincing a person of the truth that sets people free.

All this created varying and distorted pictures and expectations. So when Jesus did come as Messiah, He deliberately chose not to use the term "Messiah," and in its place chose the term "Son of Man". It wasn't because of embarrassment, nor was it an attempt to deceive, but a strategy to bring clarity as to who the Messiah was versus the distortions that abounded in the times.

Throughout history, to this day, one of the major reasons for people not to respond to the Gospel message is the distorted view of who God is; we have outlined some key points above. The need in evangelism and missions is to relate to others a proper understanding of who God is and to believe and pray for the Holy Spirit to do the inner work of convincing a person of the truth that sets people free.

At the end of the day, people reject a caricature of God or a negative religious experience more often than they adopt an outright, rebellious attitude. Our role and privilege is to share, in a clear and compassionate way, the person of God the Bible describes.

Summary:

God is our Father.

The Father loves the Son.

The Father is in heaven.

The Father has life in Himself.

The Father gives life.

The Father knows best.

The Father is always at work.

Our role and privilege is to share, in a clear and compassionate way, the person of God.

CHAPTER FIVE

Developing Cross-Cultural Communication Skills

At times, it seems that as the church, we believe it is all up to God to reach His people, that we are just pawns on a chess board in the divine process, and as long as we have the "Spirit," that is all we need.

Let me be blunt: I wonder if that attitude is just a mask for laziness. While the world waits for the answer and God offers an opportunity, we struggle along accepting mediocrity as the menu of the day. Isn't it interesting that although we work hard at getting good grades, promotions, athletic skills, there seems to be little or no specific strategy to excel in our spirituality? The Bible calls us to grow in the grace and knowledge of God, to study and show ourselves approved as a workman unto God, to live our lives as examples of the Christian life, to give ourselves to prayer, and so on. And yet we are powerless, ineffective, and poor examples.

The need has never been as great as it is now to heed the admonitions of God's Word and to begin a re-building, renewal process to line up to God's agenda. Anyone I have ever met who has been or is significant in the work of God in missions is a person who is sincere, genuine, studious, and prayerful. To one degree or another, they have done their homework. They let the destiny of God visit them and when it did, they were ready. They are much like Gideon's army, who were chosen based on their constant state of preparedness.

The thirsty soldiers of Gideon were taken to the shore of a lake; here was their chance to quench their thirst. But it was also the opportunity to test their state of preparation for battle. Some lay down and drank directly from the water, unaware of anything around them. But the ready ones were those who, on bended knee, sipped water from their cupped hands, eyes looking out for the enemy, bodies poised to bounce up at a moment's notice to engage in battle. They were chosen; the others were sent home.

As a reader of this book, you have already shown that you are, if not ready, at least ready to be made ready. You have shown your interest in mission, in preparing for cross-culturally communicating the Good News. You have begun to add tools to your arsenal for use in extreme situations, unusual opportunities to communicate God's message. This chapter will give you many more tools for the task at hand — developing effective cross-cultural communication. We'll start with simple observation.

Observe links between culture and relationship

We need to learn to observe the many ways in which the context of a culture and the relationships we seek to build are linked. To the trained eye there are thousands of cues, both little and large, begging us to pick up on them, in order that we might communicate more effectively. A singer in an opera, or an actor on a stage will always be better understood if they are supported with an appropriate set, and effective background props. In the same way, a person is better understood when seen in the context of their situation. To see how the culture and the relationship you are working on are connected is to take advantage of a much larger perspective; and this leads to much greater understanding.

> We need to learn to expand our traditional view of culture, to move from assumptions of right and wrong to an appreciation of what is different and interesting.

Expand the traditional view

We need to learn to expand our traditional view of culture, to move from assumptions of right and wrong to an appreciation of what is different and interesting.

Almost from the start, the cross cultural experience drives us to make comparisons which are perfectly normal. However, the crunch comes with what we do with our observations after we have made the comparisons. Our tendency usually is to perceive the cultural differences we observe as being right or wrong. In such a case, it is we who are wrong.

We must learn to see cultural differences as, simply, different and interesting. To use a simple illustration, in countries where people drive on the opposite side of the road, this is often described by visitors as driving on the "wrong" side of the road. This tendency to "right or wrong" judgment can escalate when culture shock is experienced; it can become very inflammatory and hurtful if not kept in check.

The reality is that these right/wrong comparisons are a defense mechanism we use when we're attempting to "get a handle" on a context in which we feel uncomfortable. However, in attempting to communicate, there is never room to make these judgmental observations.

On another level, as believers, we have determined what is right or wrong in our own culture, and when we encounter other believers in another culture who behave differently, it is easy to become self-righteous and judgmental. Once we arrive at this conclusion, the possibility of establishing any kind of relationship or communication will be lost. To suspend any judgment is crucial if we are to establish a positive, healthy relationship.

The best strategy to help us resist entering into a stuck mind-set of negativity is to work on creating positive observations in the hosting culture. It is amazing how many things one can observe, no matter how different the culture, that are interesting and perhaps even make more sense that practices in our own cultural setting.

But what if we find ourselves bogged down in a situation where cultural differences have indeed caused us to create barriers to communication? Our mission in that case is to work on conflict resolution and to reduce stress in the cross cultural experience. Remember that understanding culture and effective cross cultural communication are inseparable and must be engaged in equally.

At the lowest point possible in cross cultural communication, where a totally dysfunctional element begins to arise, and team dynamics are breaking down, personal success must become your controlling focus.

Now, let me be clear — I'm not talking about self-centered pride, or self-promoting achievement, here. I am suggesting that when your mission seems to be spiralling down into a morass of misunderstanding, you need to focus on the attitudes and actions of the one person over whose decisions you have complete control — yourself. You need to make sure that your contribution to the cross-cultural mission is everything it can be, with God's help.

…understanding
culture and effective cross cultural communication
are inseparable and must be engaged in equally.

This focus that starts right back with you and brings with it the possibility of personal health — emotionally, psychologically, and spiritually. There is no better way to begin to make a real and positive contribution to the team and culture than to maintain this level of health.

In order to develop this place of health, there are some simple principles to follow. The first is to work on being sensitive to the little, cross cultural rituals in the hosting country. To follow this protocol will ease the tension and make coping a little easier. Essentially, you will be creating significant wins in your mission; these successes will begin to create an emotional spiral up, in place of spiraling down.

The next element to build into your strategy of salvaging a negative situation is to bear down on the core value of flexibility. A strong defensive attitude creates rigidity and so, when "push comes to shove," a break point is inevitable. However, a flexible, give and take attitude will let you "live to see another day".

The third principle is to work on a proactive basis. This simply means to take initiative. Our unconsciousness self tends to back off and feel sorry for ourselves when we feel threatened. This is often called playing the victim. To be proactive is to move out from the victim mentality, to begin to work against the natural pull of human nature, to call upon the affirmations of the Word of God and the mindset it calls us to have, and to move into a positive, intentional posture. There is no need to live a life that is out of control when we have been given everything to move in exactly the opposite direction.

Jesus demonstrated a complete trust in His Father's will when at His mock trail before Pontius Pilot, He made no defense and did not demonstrate rage or revenge in the heat of the battle. He graciously accepted His Father's will and submitted to a higher authority. Culture shock expresses the very opposite. It's a result of giving in to our desire to control, confront, and conquer.

The fourth principle is to develop a transparency and a sense of vulnerability. The greatest deficit one has to operate with in cross cultural communication is an attitude of "west to the rest," in place of developing a global village attitude.

Our tendency, when we are in a funk, is to disconnect on some level, either by becoming overly aggressive and talkative, or by becoming a wallflower, and withdrawing. Both have nothing to do with communication and are destructive to the individual themselves and to the mission. The counter-punch to this situation is to utilize the extremely effective strategy of good listening habits. Positive listening habits are effective as a communication tool, as well as an opportunity for the individual who has lost their coping skills to "count to ten" before more destructive things are said or done.

Tom Peters, the very popular business guru, stated, "listening is the highest form of courtesy". In terms of our mission, listening can become a saving tool as much as a needed discipline. To listen is to communicate a clear message that the other person and what they have to say is important to you. Listening therefore validates the worth of the other person.

> The greatest deficit one has to operate with in cross cultural communication is an attitude of "west to the rest," in place of developing a global village attitude.

Some important traits and strategies in positive and effective listening include:
- Warmth and caring;
- A display of empathy;
- Demonstrating a non-judgmental attitude;
- A show of respect of the person;
- Genuineness;
- Regularly clarifying the other person's statements in order to be sure you are following and understanding them;
- Summarizing the other person's statements;
- Asking questions where appropriate;
- Not being too intrusive concerning the person's personal issues;
- Staying focused and avoiding being distracted;
- Watching for signals of an emotional nature to key in on;
- Staying away from jumping to conclusions and stereotyping.

Right Thinking Precedes Right Understanding

At some point in one's journey in missions there will be difficult or controversial issues to deal with to one degree or another. The critical success factors in overcoming and managing these issues, which can put any team and missions trip in jeopardy, include:

- Be pro-active;
- Have self-awareness to recognize the cues;
- Know how to begin spiraling upward instead of downward;
- Have a clear strategy before one gets into trouble.

> World view incorporates various levels of spirituality in the communication process. It affects individual and group self initiative, establishes core values, and impacts on decision making.

You need to ensure that you have developed an awareness of the little cultural nuances that surround you in a cross cultural situation. There is a reason cultures and people express themselves in certain ways, employing certain mannerisms. For example, to know something of the history of a culture can help you to clarify why decision-making is done in a particular way. It is important to understand something about a culture's non-verbal communication — body language, eye movement, touch, space relationships, and use of time — because all these things impact the dynamic of communicating.

Another example: to gesture with your index finger for a person to approach you is an unconscious act in our culture. However, in some cultures, this is the gesture used to call a prostitute. You definitely can get into some trouble not knowing this little tidbit of information.

Our use of body language is assimilated unconsciously

into our way of communicating. We westerners know that a turned back means rejection, folded arms and legs tend to be a defensive posture, leaning forward during conversation speaks of intense interest, leaning backward speaks of indifference. But in other cultures, these body language gestures can mean totally differing things.

In our culture, the rolling of the eyes is a statement of disbelief in a statement just heard, the opening of the eye wide indicates surprise, and so on. In other cultures, direct and lengthy eye contact can be a sign of rebellion and disdain for authority.

Touch is a personal gesture, and some may or may not appreciate the act; but generally, in our culture, it is a communication of affection or approval. In other cultures, you can be arrested for touching! Every person has a certain tolerance as to what is acceptable and not acceptable for establishing distance where comfort is not violated. In the French culture, men greet each other with a hug and two symbolic kisses, as do men in many other cultures. In some cultures, men holding hands, walking down a street, is not indicative of anything other than closeness.

Time is also cultural and someone from a time-conscious society (like ours) can easily be offended by tardiness when in reality, the other person is simply being true to a cultural norm which treats time differently. Becoming aware of all these things can dramatically enhance the success of communication.

The act that perhaps has the most impact of anything one can do is to adopt the posture of serving other people. This is close to being a cultural universal: in all countries, it is clearly understood when a person intends to express honor by serving to some degree or another.

The opposite can also be true — demonstrating humility by accepting from another culture, despite their situation or circumstance, is a powerful way to show an accepting and gracious attitude.

When it comes to expressing acceptance and graciousness toward another culture, an appreciation and understanding of the other's world view is required. The way people think, make decisions, relate, and behave is contingent upon their personal and corporate understanding of spirituality.

> The spirit of acceptance of other cultures
> and peoples is not only essential,
> but when it is evident, it expresses
> a large amount of good will toward others.

For example: I find it amazing how negotiating traffic in a busy city has changed along with spiritual changes in me. You probably find the same. Before becoming a Christian, there was no question as to the actions you would take or expressions you would make. But after becoming a Christian, even considering cutting someone off who just cut you off or slammed the brakes just ahead of you is a moral issue!

World view incorporates various levels of spirituality in the communication process. It affects individual and group self initiative, establishes core values, and impacts on decision making. Some cultures espouse an atheistic position and this very much affects how they take charge of their own lives. Others have a strong belief that each and every decision must be submitted to their deity and therefore live a more fatalistic lifestyle. Some religions have a faith that is based on prosperity and so they demonstrate a high work ethic; others rely more on the provision of God and demonstrate a more passive lifestyle.

Whatever culture you may find yourself in, the most

important principle to work on is — Do not assume you know what their belief system is or how it affects their lives. Be cautious and respectful. Consider carefully when to use proper or informal approaches to other world views. People may make statements about their own belief system, where a visitor or stranger may not!

Attitudes in Cross Cultural Communication

Our culture, especially the Christian culture, applauds the strong communicator. We have come to define success in communication in terms of the "charismatic" speaker.

Dynamic, even aggressive communication styles that are seen as successful in a secular setting are also being accepted within the church walls. We have come to expect rapid fire monologues; when the dust settles at the end of whatever we felt was important to say, we walk away feeling good about "communicating" — although I suspect the communication is often one-way. If that.

Other cultures see things differently and accept more readily an approach that allows more dialogue. When communicating, there is a happy medium between capitulating and being too apologetic, and coming across too strong. The best concept to keep in mind is the "peach philosophy" of communicating, which positions itself "firm and sweet." One of the more effective approaches is to initiate praise and affirmation wherever possible and appropriate. But always, be honest! The danger is to overdo it and move into flattery, which can patronize others. The rule is to follow the KISS principle ... keep it simple, stupid!

Sometimes it seems ironic — as humans, we are actually better equipped for successful cross-cultural communication than we permit ourselves to be. We all have a number of traits, natural to human nature, which under pressure are easily forgotten. Then, of course, they are of no use to us.

For example, we all come with a certain level of inquisitiveness. An attitude of inquisitiveness, leading you to ask many sincere questions, can lead to many good experiences and successful outcomes.

As creations of God, we also come with a certain supply of openness to others. The spirit of acceptance of other cultures and peoples is not only essential, but when it is evident, it expresses a large amount of good will toward others.

Personal stability, or health, is also important. When you can demonstrate stability — emotionally, psychologically, and spiritually — this allows others to feel comfortable and have easy access to you as to someone who is "safe". Instability in any area is perceived as unsafe and unpredictable, and predictability is a deep human need.

An air of proficiency is also an attractive element to have. When others perceive a sense of depth and excellence, they will be attracted you you and to your message.

A high level of motivation is also an attitude that is contagious, and a precious trait to hold. If you were to begin at any place, in developing strong cross cultural communication skills or life success skills generally, this is where to start! Simply performing and evaluating a self-audit around these traits will reveal core values and strengths that can be worked on to enable you to excel.

Know your environmental enemies

The four enemies of a healthy environment in cross cultural communication are hunger, anger, loneliness, and fatigue. These serve well as a thermometer to check your well-being.

- Stay healthy with nutritional food.
- Deal with anger issues.
- Resist the loneliness trap by engaging regularly with others.

- Avoid fatigue whenever possible, and create a strategy for coping at the times where it is inevitable.

> When you sign up for team missions, you are committed and expected to work on being relational, accepting, and supportive, no matter what.

Summary:

Stress management and the development of an emotional strength go hand in hand when working with a team and communicating cross culturally.

Participating in creating a positive atmosphere is essential. There may be situations where a designated time and place is established to work through the tough issues, and it would be detrimental not to do so. However, when engaged in missions it is important to do your part in keeping things on the up side. Focus on why you are there and for Whom you are doing what you do. That focus on the Great Commissioner should serve to ensure a positive attitude.

You are part of a team. When you sign up for team missions, you are committed and expected to work on being relational, accepting, and supportive, no matter what. Team play is a crucial aspect of enjoying the journey when on missions, and it is the responsibility of each member to seek out ways to develop a warm and fun environment.

Seizing the time you have and making the most of it is also important. There is only so much time, and to wallow in negativity, conflict, and withdrawal is not the best use of it, to say the least. Issues will heal and relationships will be patched up but unfortunately, the time consumed in not moving forward on the field is not a renewable resource and can never be retrieved. So take advantage of the time and deal with it!

Sometimes the best policy is to remind yourself that this is what you signed up for, and you're on the bus, so stay on and make the best of it, even if it does not always meet your expectations. Remember, your responsibility when you're on a team is the team itself, not you as an individual. This means that you forfeit many of your individual rights for the better of the team. Our culture does not understand this principle and would do well with a large dose of it. A high level of tolerance is the order of the day while on a team and in a cross-cultural experience. Begin to learn to accept that difference is a fact and not a negative, but a contribution to the health of the team.

It is important to be principle-centered; however, to be rigid to the point where a break happens more often than flexing means there is a problem.

CHAPTER SIX

The Eleven Mindsets Required for Cross-Cultural Communication

Christianity, by definition, is paradoxical. A paradox is a truth that presents itself as the opposite of the popular, common understanding of the day. For example, Jesus calls upon believers to die so they will find life; He tells us that to be great in His Kingdom we must be the least here; and He says that giving a cup of cold water to someone in need is giving it to Him.

Cross cultural communications is also a paradox, in that in order to be truly effective the person going into the cross cultural context must :

a) unlearn everything they ever thought they knew about communicating,

b) become aware of the dynamic of communicating,

c) take the initiative in the communication exercise, and

d) learn as much as possible in order to approach cross cultural communication as if you had everything to learn and knew nothing.

So all of one's life is spent learning and picking up the survival skills of communication, both consciously and unconsciously. Then, when it seems that all your acquired skills are just the prescription for achieving the goal of effective communication, you're told that the rules are all changed and more learning is essential. In this chapter we will attempt to overcome the confusing and somewhat frustrating paradox in cross-cultural communication. The principles are of inestimable value in achieving a successful and effective outcome in a cross-cultural context.

Definition of Presupposition: "to require something as prior condition. To make something necessary if a particular thing is to be shown to be true or false." Another current word for "presupposition" can be "mindset."

We want to be successful in reaching others with the gospel. Therefore, we need to have the enlightenment and understanding that there are certain things we need to know and to do, in order to make a way for others to be more open to the message. Paul states in 1 Corinthians that he "became all things to all people so that by all means some might become saved." Unfortunately, in our day this approach to reaching others with the gospel is often rejected as "a compromise" or "outright sin".

This is based in an unfortunate misunderstanding. Of course, as followers of Christ, we are not to compromise with sin. The end never justifies improper means.

But the problem here lies in a judgmental attitude that classifies external, cultural issues as sin. Let's always be sure to let the Bible — not extra-biblical rules — alert us to what sin is. A good place to start would be the seven letters to the churches in the book of Revelation; there, we are given a good introduction to a Christian understanding of sin.

> The decision that you now must make is: are you are going to excel at your choice or are you going to live a life of mediocrity, satisfied with half-hearted attempts at doing something that really requires excellence

Stephen R. Covey, in his best-selling book, "The Seven Habits of Highly Effective People," says that in order to be understood you must work first on understanding the other person. The challenge in actually accomplishing this is that our cultural baggage can get in the way. Or, our understanding of spirituality can simply not allow us to "go there".

Another basic block to becoming a more effective cross-cultural communicator is that, frankly, it takes a lot of work. There is no half-hearted way to do the right thing. To become effective for the Kingdom, we must become students of the Bible, of ourselves, and of others. Once you determine to reach the lost — let alone to embark upon missions — you cease to live with the privileged notion that you can just be a "sanctuary" person. A "sanctuary" person is one who sees no need to do or know anything besides what happens to them in a

Mission_Shift

Sunday service. They work, play, attend church services, and live their lives out with relatively little sense of urgency when it comes to the affairs of the Kingdom of God. Nothing is necessarily wrong with the sanctuary life, it's just not the road you have chosen to take at this time in your life.

> These excellent leaders shared characteristics including extreme commitment, extreme flexibility, and extreme vision. As believers we are all involved in leadership at some level; this demands the same "extremes" of us.

The decision that you now must make is: are you are going to excel at your choice or are you going to live a life of mediocrity, satisfied with half-hearted attempts at doing something that really requires excellence.

Leaders often make a fundamental error. They attempt to recruit numbers instead of motivated individuals; in their efforts to achieve certain levels of quantity, they lose out in the area of quality. These kind of recruitment efforts lead to lots of "warm bodies" and not nearly enough men and women with a passion for Christ and the lost, who desire to arrive at competency and spiritual levels in their lives beyond the status quo.

One story about Alexander the Great suggests that when he wasn't leading the charge and fighting a war, he would entertain himself by holding kangaroo court. People would be brought forward to him with all kinds of accusations and he would decide their fate. One day a sentry was brought to him who had been found sleeping at his post. Being derelict in duty enraged Alexander. He asked the soldier what his name was and the soldier answered that his name was Alexander. At this news Alexander the Great jumped from his judgement chair, drew his sword, brought it down to the soldier's neck and said, "Young man, change your conduct or change your name!"

When we step up to being involved in missions, we are carrying the name of Christ. We therefore are also taking upon ourselves the responsibility to change our conduct. That's the mindset that needs to be created within us — the desire and commitment to change our conduct. Too often we accept step one without step two — we involve ourselves in something with no intention of shifting our attitudes, behavior, or conduct.

The ground-breaking book, "The Leader of the Present" published by the Peter Drucker Foundation, shares some very basic but essential discoveries about excellent leaders. These excellent leaders shared characteristics including extreme commitment, extreme flexibility, and extreme vision. As believers we are all involved in leadership at some level; this demands the same "extremes" of us.

Developing compatibility

The first mindset to communicating cross-culturally is: when working in a differing culture, job one is to work on developing compatibility. As believers, we tend to be cause-based. We clearly see the driving need to lead someone to make a decision, but our fundamental focus on the end can tend to blind us to other, more immediate issues. A certain myopic dynamic enters in, causing us to not take into account terms, cues, feelings or perceptions of others. This "short and straight to the point" approach usually leads to a sense that the other person is an object to be conquered and that we are out to win a crusade. (By the way, if you do only the most basic study of the word "crusade", you will realize that both this attitude, and this term itself, are very culturally insensitive concepts to apply to reaching out in the love of Christ.)

Throughout the Gospels, we see in the ministry of Jesus a

far different approach. There seemed to be no "hurry up offense" in His life or ministry. What is shown is a compassionate, deliberate desire to love unconditionally and to respect others. From the choosing of the twelve disciples, to His meeting with the woman at the well, to the woes pronounced upon the religious leaders, Jesus demonstrated an interest in others regardless of their situation, position, or opposition.

The disciples were dealt with on the basis that although they had a lot to learn and understand, Jesus still supported them and sent them out in the power of the Holy Spirit.

> ...expressing yourself in the way that is usual and acceptable "back home" may not necessarily be the usual and acceptable way in the culture you are visiting.

The woman at the well was gently led along a line of discussion that moved from her familiar tradition, to religious beliefs, to spiritual leadership, to the place where she came to — and owned — her own conclusion about who Jesus was. This patient process eventually led to a person who went on to share the good news, herself.

The woes Jesus pronounced were statements of regret, not angry lashing out at "you evil people" as we have come to commonly understand. Remember that Jesus gazed over Jerusalem one day and wept for the city because of its refusal to understand who He was and what a difference He could make had the people of the city accepted Him and his mission.

When embarking on missions or cross-cultural communication, the beginning, middle, and end of the work that needs to be done is that of overcoming differences, discovering areas of common ground, and identifying essential and non-essential issues. Allowing insecurity to seep in, or adopting a bunker mentality that leads to vilifying anyone who disagrees with us, only ends up in hurting the cause, hurting the intended recipient, and hurting ourselves. The premise of the "wounded healer" is that the wounded one must first be healed of the emotional damage. Only when we are secure in our own healing will we come to a point where we don't have an axe to grind with others, but a message to share.

Customs, thought processes and social systems vary

The second mindset in cross-cultural communication is that customs, thought processes and social systems vary greatly from culture to culture. The initial idea of "going global" sounds exciting and exotic, and our emotions can run ahead of us, as we overlook the task of working towards building mutually respectful relationships in order to engage in meaningful and effective communication.

To state it simply, expressing yourself in the way that is usual and acceptable "back home" may not necessarily be the usual and acceptable way in the culture you are visiting. And unless you have done your homework, you may not realize the mistake you are making. Your hosts may overlook your particular approach and respond graciously, but this doesn't mean that you have not caused offense. In truth, offense may have been taken, but for the host to have taken issue with it at the time may have been culturally unacceptable, or there may be a different underlying reason for not speaking out or confronting the issue.

Even in our "open and honest" culture in North America we are not so eager to share the brutal facts. Think about the last time you had a poor meal in a restaurant; what did you tell the server when he or she asked "How was your meal?" Odds are good, you said, "Fine, thanks," and then decided never to eat there again. Usually, we would rather "vote with our feet" and just avoid any confrontation.

In a cross-cultural situation, Christians must be well prepared and keenly sensitive to customs that may be displayed that could create a break or barrier in developing a relationship.

How one processes information can also have an impact, positively or negatively. It is important to be aware of how a culture takes in information and draws conclusions.

Truthfully, to be in a different culture and be able to avoid absolutely all offenses would be impossible. However, having some of your homework done in this area will lead to a more effective and positive experience. In the social setting, expressions, behaviors, and interactions can be vastly different from culture to culture. But we can create a greater opportunity to become successful in the cross-cultural experience. With effort and commitment, learning how to socially interact is both achievable and rewarding.

Reacting to each situation

The third mindset in cross-cultural communication is that you will either react or respond to each situation. You need to understand this; believing that you can accept a new situation without instinctively reacting will only lead to problems. As you understand your own potential reactions, you can prepare to manage them, and choose instead to respond, in the power of the Holy Spirit.

Our most dangerous elemental impulses is to experience a "flight" or "fight" reaction. Once the cross-cultural "difference" is perceived — whether it be a custom, process, or social circumstance — the reaction of the inexperienced and unlearned may be "flight" — to falter in insecurity and want save oneself by running away from the situation. This will instantly cut off communication.

Or, the reaction may be "fight" — to take on the situation, head-on, and mask your insecurity by an aggressive response to the culture shock. In truth, either option, fight or flight, is negative unless one's life is in jeopardy!

The difference between the negative, "reaction" mode of dealing with a situation cross-culturally, and a "response," is that the responsive posture can lead to a positive outcome. The responsive stance is one that analyzes the situation, taps into an internal motivation to want to communicate, and seeks creative ways to enhance the communication process.

In a cross-cultural situation, Christians must be well prepared and keenly sensitive to customs that may be displayed that could create a break or barrier in developing a relationship.

The key is to recognize that success in cross-cultural communication depends on seeing differences as resources and not as threats to one's person. Once we become defensive and take "stuck" situations personally, the spiral down to a total dysfunction in communicating has begun. This downward spiral begins with the perceived difference between the two cultures, then moves toward a sense of unease, then stress. This stress is what triggers the desire to either fight or take flight and withdraw from the situation. At this point nothing positive results.

One response, in place of reactive surrendering to the predictable dynamic of "losing it," is to begin to think in terms of creating a third culture that is neither assimilation into the other's culture (which is practically impossible) or a cocooning into your own culture (which is a major withdrawal from the cross-cultural event). This third culture is a "safe" place where both parties or groups can go in order to develop a strategy to focus on the outcomes of success and effectiveness.

> The key is to recognize
> that success in cross-cultural communication
> depends on seeing differences as resources
> and not as threats to one's person.

This approach is applicable in any context where communication is required. We need to recognize and understand that exact copies of ourselves can only multiply our own flaws; and that the differences of other people, groups, and cultures can prove to be a valuable resource to understanding.

Relationship building is the key to communication

The fourth mindset in cross-cultural communication is that relationship building is the vital key to creating a positive outcome in communication. When we, in a previous chapter, dealt with the concept of believers being ambassadors, it was evident that representation and relationship are the supporting structures for effective biblical communication with others. To be on guard against abandoning this prescription will lead to a more positive and fluid experience when communicating cross-culturally.

When relationships are healthy, we tend to judge people by their motives and intentions rather than their actions. This simply means that in good relationships, we begin by assuming the same about others as we would want them to assume about us ... the very best! Relationship building also creates a deposit in the "bank of goodwill;" a healthy relationship has a balance in the account that can stand withdrawals once in a while, when a mistake is made. Relationship building is the lubricant that decreases friction when the pressure is on and the going gets a little tough. If tolerance is the byword, then relationship is the instrument to create the tolerance everyone is looking for.

Information exchange is a consequence of relationship

The fifth mindset to cross-cultural communication is that information exchange must be seen as a consequence of relationship. The old adage — people don't care what you know until they know that you care — comes into play here. Only once a relationship foundation has been laid can real information processing, and information exchange happen. In situations where time is of the essence, is it easy to violate this principle. However, if we ignore the need for relationship, nothing will be accomplished anyway.

When training teams for missions, there is always a place where dealing with time constraints is discussed. There are some very simple yet effective principles that need to be followed.

The first is — the person communicating is the person responsible for effective strategies for success. This means that it takes work and preparation for the individual who must take seriously what he or she is doing.

The second is — nothing effective happens outside a "divine appointment" with another person. This is where one realizes that the encounter is set up by God. Prayer, discernment, sensitivity and the leading of the Holy Spirit are essential to an encounter in communication. This can be accomplished with one person or thousands, depending on the gifts, opportunities, and context God has placed someone in to minister.

Third — when an encounter is established, that situation

is the place one's focus, energy, and time need to be poured into.

And lastly — relationship building is still the centerpiece to a short encounter. When we are on the streets, in a cross-cultural situation, God is moving by His Holy Spirit, and insurmountable odds are being overcome. Time and again, connections have been divinely created where in normal terms, there was insufficient time. In a very compressed segment of time, a relationship was established, communication was created, and an openness that led to a very effective encounter resulted.

A great biblical example is that story of the woman at the well, who had a conversation with Jesus. In one conversation between two strangers, one encountered a personal relationship with God, was transformed in her own self perception, and was motivated to share the good news with her whole community. It can happen during a short plane ride, in a meeting, at an event. It is a very exciting experience, keeping an openness and anticipation for a divine appointment.

No communication without understanding

The sixth mindset in cross-cultural communication is that there is no communication without understanding of the person's cross-cultural process. When communicating generally and internationally, success always boils down to knowing, "it's not what you say but how you say it!" As well, "it's not always what you say but it's how the receiver sees you as a person".

As a person, as a communicator, as a believer with a message, you are a brand! A "brand" is the product signature someone else sees that either attracts or repels him or her from pursuing a deeper interest. A brand is what a person recognizes before what is inside is more fully revealed.

The three elements to branding are: competencies, standards, and style. Often we confuse the three and end up misrepresenting ourselves, our product, or our message.

"Competencies" represent your role in life — parent, scientist, etc.

"Standards" are like core values, the "how you do something" aspect. This addresses the integrity, excellence, or efficiency of doing something.

"Style" is how the message about the product is communicated.

> As a person, as a communicator, as a believer with a message, you are a brand!

Competencies and standards are well established in the Bible. Our competencies in our roles as believers are empowered by the Holy Spirit. Our standards are clear — to love, to be like Christ. The New Testament is very clear about the competencies and standards inherent in our mission.

But "style" is a totally different matter. Sometimes, due to our orientation that is established by our particular spiritual experience, we adopt styles we have been brought up with or influenced by and take them as non-negotiables for communicating. We feel to a great extent that if a particular, familiar style is not used consistently, we somehow compromise the truth. For example, should someone be asked to speak at a Sunday service and come across as a rather mundane, non-eventful communicator, they may be categorized as not having the "anointing" where perhaps they simply lack dynamic communication skills.

On the other hand should someone communicate like the proverbial "house on fire," they may be deemed as "anointed" when in reality they may simply be a talented speaker accomplished in public speaking.

At the end of the day, the morality, integrity, and sincerity of the person is the benchmark for the "anointing". Theologically, we could visit this issue and truly have our spiritual lens re-focused! Suffice it to say that the "anointing" is the empowerment of the Holy Spirit to be able to live a morally supernatural life.

The message will change the relationship

Mindset number seven is that the message you are attempting to communicate will change the relationship, depending upon the content and acceptance of the message. Let's be honest at this point, and understand not everyone is going to blissfully accept what a missionary has to say. They will disagree based upon prejudice, religion, and culture. The Bible is loaded with the reality that rejection, ignorance, resistance, and even persecution are part and parcel of the response to the Christian message. As a matter of fact Paul the apostle says that all who desire to live a godly life will suffer persecution. How about that for a memory verse?

Our current church culture seems to suggest that we are God's gift to humanity and that everyone will just openly accept the Gospel . That somehow there is a sense of entitlement to an easy road of ministry if we only believe. Not so! The nature of our future relationship with others will be based on their acceptance or rejection of the message we are communicating. We may have a growing relationship, or we may suffer a disconnection.

The message changes with the credibility of the one giving it

Mindset number eight is of significant importance, for it has to do with our willingness to adjust, to work to ensure that, as much as possible we are not the reason for the rejection of the message. This rule states that the message you give changes with the perception of the credibility of the person giving it. Straight up, this means that we can either contribute to the effectiveness of the message or we can be a roadblock. Attitudes, presentation, non-verbal messages, dress, style, sincerity, and so on are all up for negotiation when communicating. Remember Paul the apostle's statement that he became all things to all people so that by all means some might be saved? A close and honest self examination is called for if we are to move on to the ultimate outcome in cross-cultural communication. That desired outcome is, of course, to successfully and effectively reach someone else with our message.

> The nature of our future relationship with others will be based on their acceptance or rejection of the message we are communicating.

The message changes with the perception of similarity

The ninth mindset is that the message changes with the hearer's perception of similarity with the person giving the message. In other words the person being communicated to, by you, is also looking for signs and cues to see if there is any compatibility, and to find some common ground they can work with.

This ongoing dynamic is why we must work toward understanding another culture and/or another person. This is the reason why anyone seeking to communicate cross-culturally must study the recipients of the message. There is, in a very real sense, a non-verbal dance going on involving both parties — one, the speaker, trying to connect the message to something understandable, and one, the hearer, attempting to connect it with something they are familiar with. When this connection occurs, communication happens and the potential for a relationship is struck.

> …anyone seeking to communicate cross-culturally must study the recipients of the message.

The best way to take advantage of this principle is to understand and appreciate how another culture processes information in tangible and non-verbal ways, and then to attempt to work those processes into the delivery of the message. In psychological terms this is called "mirroring". Mirroring is the active study of how another person's body language, style, and thinking work, and attempting to relate to them using the same mannerisms. For example, using chop sticks to eat in an Asian culture can convey a sense that you are attempting to respect their culture. This often creates a desire on the other person's part to invest the same amount of energy in communicating on some level.

Your style affects communication

Number ten mindset is that your preference or style for communicating affects communication. Your own cultural baggage dictates how your thinking process works, how you behave socially, whether you are dominant or passive in your personality. It affects how sympathetic you are, or how indifferent you are. It determines if you are a take-charge person who tends to be a lone ranger in your style, or someone who works on a more cooperative level. It determines whether your general approach to life is easy-going and distracted, or rigid and focused.

All this baggage, when taken into another culture, can become assets or liabilities. Assets are those aspects of your personal culture that work in your favor in communicating; liabilities are those aspects that work to your disadvantage in communicating cross-culturally.

The key here is to understand the cultural baggage you are carrying with you. When taken for granted, both the positive and negative aspects of your cultural style are automatically expressed when you are communicating. The discipline of becoming aware of these particular aspects of your being, and the application of them in a positive sense, is all part of the call to servanthood and discipleship.

Cross-cultural communication is very stressful

Number eleven mindset is that cross-cultural communication is a very stressful and demanding exercise. It must not be taken lightly or glibly; you would be completely wrong to believe that you are unique and that the stress of cross-cultural communication doesn't or won't affect you.

Denial, ignorance, and dismissal of the emotional and psychological trauma are actually among the signs of culture shock. The best posture to take, no matter how much experience you have cross-culturally and no matter how much experience you have in a team dynamic, is the "high road" of humility. You may be able to help other team members because of your previous experience; however, you must remember that each and every trip overseas or into another culture is different, calling upon differing skills to allow you to compensate and overcome situations. That is why it's called dynamic.

The best de-stresser approach is:
- to accept that we do experience stress;

- to gather intelligence on how you specifically become stressed;

> The best posture to take, no matter how much experience you have cross-culturally and no matter how much experience you have in a team dynamic, is the "high road" of humility.

- to identify the psychological and physical signs of stress in your life;
- to learn as much as you can about stress and coping mechanisms;
- to learn as much as you can about the symptoms of stress in your team; and
- to create a strategy to manage stress in your life during a cross-cultural experience.

Remember, stress is a fact. Stress is something that can ever be totally eliminated, so it must be managed. The three significant catalysts for stress are called the "F.U.D.s" — Fear, Uncertainty, and Doubt. The cross-cultural experience will always bring on these driving and sabotaging emotions, to one degree or another. There will be fear of rejection by another person, uncertainty over how it's all going to work out, and the impending negativity created by insecurity. There will always be confusion and ambiguity in cross-cultural communication and the better prepared one is, the more effective one can be.

One hundred per cent success is improbable, but the elimination of as much F.U.D. as possible is the goal. Perhaps the best way to understand the dynamics of the F.U.D. in one's life is by using the "blind date" scenario. The less you know about the other person, the more seems to be on the line. There is little or no opportunity to "size up" the other person. You don't know what they like, what they are attracted to in another person, or what style they like; you are flying blind. The anticipation, the first sight and the first few words are all like nails sliding down a chalk board, until there comes a sense of compatibility and common ground.

Most of us have relationships with people we originally met under circumstances like that. But now, you have known each other for a long time, and you understand each other on many levels. How simple it now seems. When you meet today, there is no anxiety, and there is instant and deep communication.

That's the goal in cross-cultural communication; to get from the "blind date" to the comfortable relationship.

It will be helpful to always remember other times in life when that transition was made successfully. The higher the predictability and the greater the clarity, the more comfort one has in the cross-cultural communication process. On a rather simplistic level, the less the need for guess work in communication, the greater sense of comfort one has.

> There will always be confusion and
> ambiguity in cross-cultural communication
> and the better prepared one is,
> the more effective one can be.

Therefore, to repeat a truth stated more than once in this book, as you develop familiarity with the other culture or person, you will lower the level the less stress you will encounter. In essence, you are developing a framework so that you can understand, process, and anticipate how the other culture or person will function.

This is not entirely foreign territory — we have all had plenty of experience in trying to understand and anticipate the communication of others. Think of a school exam, or the brief, mid-game directions of an athletic coach — there is a constant deciphering of the expectations of the teacher or the coach as to what they want from you at any given time.

> The more information gathering done at the beginning of the trip, the better prepared you are going to be, and the more effective and successful you will become.

In those situations, you invest time not only in knowing the content of the exam, or the position to be played, but you also give consideration to the nuances — what the teacher is specifically looking for in an answer, or the level of play in the opposing team. The same goes for cross-cultural communication. The more information gathering done at the beginning of the trip, the better prepared you are going to be, and the more effective and successful you will become.

So, while cross-cultural communication will never be cut-and-dried, and can never be predicted by a formula, there are a number of presuppositions or mindsets that will help you to be prepared. And thus, to be more successful. You can work on taking the guess work out of the communication process; you must develop greater familiarity of the culture; you should go through the process of information gathering and overcoming superficial introductions; you should prepare yourself to expect situations much like a "first date" experience. All this preparation will contribute to a successful cross-cultural communication process, and increase the potential for a successful conclusion.

If you have chosen to engage in missions and cross-cultural communications, the only issue left to be resolved is how much work are you going to put into it, and to what level of excellence are you ready to go? There is no wrong way to do a right thing!

A few suggestions to get the ball rolling in the area of developing cross-cultural communication aptitude:

• Create a covenant with yourself, in writing, that expresses your determination to excel to the best of your abilities in the area of understanding others before your needs are met. Express your understanding that a posture of humility with others will be a critical success factor. Include a set of personal values to live by, containing elements from the presuppositions outlined in this chapter.

• Write a hypothetical letter to another culture, communicating your desire to be compatible with them, and stating specific ways in which you intend to be successful with your intention.

• Write a prayer to God asking Him to guide you through the process in the best way possible to reflect His glory and to represent Him.

• Establish a personal priority list from the eleven presuppositions is a creative and positive way to begin engaging in the material, in order for you assimilate it into your being.

• From a leadership position, establish how you would want your team to behave as they travel and work cross-culturally.

These ideas, as well as other creative ways to interact with the material, will go a long way to help you prayerfully prepare yourself for a successful cross-cultural communication event.

Summary:

Eleven mindsets required for cross-cultural communication:

- When working in a differing culture, job one is to work on developing compatibility.
- Customs, thought processes and social systems vary greatly from culture to culture.
- You will either react or respond to each situation.
- Relationship building is the vital key to creating a positive outcome in communication.
- Information exchange must be seen as a consequence of relationship.
- There is no communication without understanding of the person's cross-cultural process.
- The message you are attempting to communicate will change the relationship, depending upon the content and acceptance of the message.
- The message you give changes with the perception of the credibility of the person giving it.
- The message changes with the hearer's perception of similarity with the person giving the message.
- Your preference or style for communicating affects communication.
- Cross-cultural communication is a very stressful and demanding exercise.

CHAPTER SEVEN

The Global Reality and the Global Opportunity

Global communications are at a point far beyond anything humanity has known in the past. The images instantly conveyed to every part of the globe are powerful and pervasive.

Because they are always and immediately available, the key images of our time are etched in my mind, even though some of the pivotal, historical events took place while I was travelling in some of the most remote parts of the world. I was always able to catch up with current world news events, courtesy of CNN.

I'm thinking of images of the Berlin Wall being dismantled, leading to the reunification of East and West Germany. The images of people celebrating, people who had lived under the oppression of communism for seventy years. Some of those images I recall from first-hand experience, as I drove through Eastern European countries where the symbols of an ideology were being torn down, where crowds were freely meeting in public square after public square.

This was a time where it seemed the "good guys" were winning the war of socio-cultural dominance, where Western world lifestyle, freedom, and religious beliefs were gaining more and more ground. The economy was picking up speed; it hit a fevered pitch with the dot-com boom, and created a sense of invincibility and permanence. Then came the dot-com bust, a down-turn in the economy ensued and, in an explosion that felt like a closing crescendo, 9-11 happened, shaking our sense of security and well-being to the roots.

At the end of the day, fear, uncertainty, and doubt seem to have been revealed as the controlling emotions lying just beneath the surface of our hectic, preoccupied lives. Coping skills have thinned out. In a desperate appeal to our own senses, we engage in motion but realize no movement forward. Hoping to crowd out the real questions of life, we settle for a superficial social agenda. And in place of meaningful dialog, we offer opinions on issues that, at the end of the day, matter not at all.

What has surfaced in these times is a new and terrifying understanding of the reality that difference exists. It exists in our political, social, ethnic, and religious spheres. While we endorsed "can't we all just get along," and "give peace a chance," the truth is that, deep down in the human spirit, an insecurity lives that whispers that we cannot simply well-wish the challenges of life away.

Our responses to those whispers have been many and varied. A multitude of "religions" have flourished; some have even been lately invented. This "pluralism" is not the agenda of an activist group, but the byproduct of attempting to create unity through the process of reducing the complexities of life to the lowest common denominator. What is left is a prevailing attitude that there is a spiritual cafeteria offering a whole menu of belief systems. One can choose, and all choices are good. It is a sure thing ... no one loses! However, this has never been the truth as demonstrated by Christ. I quoted C.S. Lewis earlier pointing out that Christianity is an exclusive faith. This does not mean God wants to exclude anyone; it does mean that belief in Christ excludes belief in other religious systems.

> What has surfaced in these times
> is a new and terrifying understanding of the reality that
> difference exists. It exists in our political, social, ethnic,
> and religious spheres.

We have reached a point in our society where we believe that choice is a personal issue, not for public consumption. Values are lived out without comment by another. While that seems humane and even noble, it leaves room for all manner of excesses — all justified by personal freedom and privacy. We have an ethos where extreme ends of the pendulum are represented and are expressed freely.

The factors contributing to this "anything goes" sense of spirituality include the "Global Village" situation created by the mobility, availability, and technology dynamics that exist today. The religious activity of other faiths world-wide offer up options that did not exist, and the number of multi-faith communities are on the rise.

All of this has left Christianity on the retreat, gutted in its core, or sympathetic to a position where ecumenicalism seems like "a good thing". Today, Jesus is one option among many, and to claim exclusiveness, as noted above, leads to a charge not new in history — that Christianity is bigoted, intolerant, and mean-spirited. Sadly, in honesty we must confess that throughout history, people claiming the name "Christian" have indeed at times been bigoted, intolerant, and mean-spirited. But — I must stress this, here — those vices did not arise because the truth of Christianity is exclusive; it arose because they wrongly tried to keep Christianity for their exclusive, personal edification.

In a way it is simply understood: Christianity is entirely inclusive, in that "God so loved the world." It is exclusive because Jesus is the only "way, the truth, the life." Everyone is invited into the Kingdom, but there is only one "Door."

But many in the global village seem unwilling to accept this. Those of us who have encountered Jesus in a personal way, and have come to know Him as "The Way, The Truth, and The Life," seem ill equipped to take on such a seemingly insurmountable mountain of resistance. However, the same Person who claimed to be the Way also commissioned His followers to "Go into all the world and make disciples".

What is needed between the "Aha!" of encounter and the "Yes" to the Great Commission is a realization that a strategic approach is required, as well as the experience and anointing provided by God. Despite the litany of challenges listed above (and by no means is this an exhaustive list), there are pillars of support that can lift our spirits, set our gaze, and galvanize our resolve to carry on the torch passed onto to us by "a great cloud of witnesses".

The first pillar is the recognition that the Church lives in what I call a "post modern advantage". What is this advantage? It is the realization that the anti-supernatural doctrine of the Enlightenment has been dissolved. Even though faith does not seem necessary, it is also not dismissed out of hand. This creates a certain level playing field, and opens dialogue between beliefs and faiths allowing expression of one's world view.

The second pillar of support is the availability of information at a speed and volume never thought possible. Neil Postman, in his book "The End of Education," makes an amazing statement when he says that, never in the history of human civilization has there been more information outside the classroom than in the classroom.

The information age has provided the potential for anyone with a computer and internet access to find themselves in a sea of information with the pressing of a key. In the early nineties I found myself fascinated with this revolution, where no longer was power held by the withholding of information

> The term defense
> literally means "apology" — not meaning
> an apology for a wrong done,
> but to provide a logical, reasonable explanation
> for why you believe in Christ as Lord.

nor the "early bird" getting the worm and being "beaten out" on an opportunity, but where flood gates were opened and information was instantly available to the person at the outermost edge of the world. Before I left one position to move across the country, over thirty percent of my books were left behind and CD ROMs and my Explorer Favorite sites replaced them. Only a few years later, more and more of my research and information are accessed via technology. One intriguing example — scriptures quoted in this book were not typed into the manuscript by hand; they were sourced on the net, and downloaded as text. Amazing!

Why is this availability of information a strategic pillar of support? Because the believers need to have information available; in cross-cultural communication, we require a level of knowledge that can be used to create common ground with another person, to express interest, and to defend one's faith.

Peter says in one of his letters that the Christian should always be prepared to make a defense for the reason they believe. The term defense literally means "apology" — not meaning an apology for a wrong done, but to provide a logical, reasonable explanation for why you believe in Christ as Lord.

We are always to be ready to share our faith, and to be harmless as doves and wise as serpents. The clearer we are concerning our own definition of Christianity, the more effective we will be.

A third pillar of support for the Christian in the postmodern world is to realize that high ideas are influencing the status quo. We are living in a time where a window is open through which we can speak to the questions and concerns people have. There is a conundrum — while there seems to be a rise in the immorality of society, there is equally a higher respect for those who desire and strive to live a morally high life. The condition to this respect is for the individual to have a clear reason for this stance.

This leads to a fourth pillar of support — Jesus is actually an option today. At first hearing, this may sound like a rather trite statement. However, this pillar speaks to the open door of opportunity the believer has to take advantage of. There is a willingness on the part of others to discuss, debate, and consider the claims of Jesus; this openness allows the Holy Spirit to do His special work of grace. In order to take advantage of this open door, however, there needs to be recognition of the need to "grow in the grace and knowledge" of the Lord Jesus Christ as the apostle Peter says.

Note that the process of growth is two-fold. One is to grow both in grace, and knowledge. It is amazing how much respect, effectiveness, and results you can get by showing just a little initiative in the area of actually enhancing the information you have to support your belief system.

Pillar number five is good news when one stops to consider how Christianity has been dismissed in the past. The fact that in this postmodern society, all religions are considered equal, creates a positive edge for the believer. In other words, to discuss religion is fair game and to speak of Christianity is part of the discussion. Any way that Christianity can be inserted into a discussion is an opportunity to share the truth, to present Christ's claims for consideration.

Pillar six is something that has been present ever since the creation of man, but which has been denied in an intellectually suppressed time. This pillar realizes that human beings are implicitly believers. Today, for the first time in decades, perhaps centuries, society openly accepts that belief is a valid, deeply seated, closely-held concept. This positions the believer in a place of inherent integrity. A reaction of thoughtless ridicule is much less common today, and we can take advantage of situations to share Christ.

We are always to be ready to share our faith, and to be harmless as doves and wise as serpents. The clearer we are concerning our own definition of Christianity, the more effective we will be. The Bible, from Genesis to Revelation, has as a central theme — the story of a God who loves His creation, even though they chose to reject Him and go their own way. This choice led to a broken relationship, which God has been desiring to restore, ever since. Paul declared in his letters to Timothy that God is not willing for anyone to perish, but for all to come to a knowledge of Him. Ultimately, through God

Mission_*Shift*

becoming man in Jesus and dying on the cross, He took our place of judgment and removed the condemning result. He did this freely and offers this gift of life freely.

Good News — which is the word we use for evangelism — is all about this theme. Good News that Jesus took our consequences of death and eternal separation upon Himself; Good News that Jesus offers life here and now; Good News that we can share this message and help others escape from suffering a needless, eternal separation from God.

> As we journey through life and continue to discover the amazing grace of Jesus in our lives, let us recognize the need to prepare ourselves to take advantage of the door of opportunity before us, to reach just one person. Let's remember that the tool of choice Jesus wants to use is the sold-out individual who shows up, day after day, as a faithful and obedient follower of Christ.

Christianity is not about religious ritual, doctrinal obedience, nor some kind of cultic suppression, it is about relationship, unconditional love, forgiveness, community, grace, and acceptance. Christianity is about establishing a moral standard whereby the mandate of Jesus to us, to let our good works so shine before man that they will see our good works and glorify our Father in Heaven, is carried out. It is about reflecting absolutes in a world where everything is relative.

As we journey through life and continue to discover the amazing grace of Jesus in our lives, let us recognize the need to prepare ourselves to take advantage of the door of opportu-

The Global Reality and the Global Opportunity

nity before us, to reach just one person. After all the revivals, after all the events, after all the programs and special appearances of the "wonderfully gifted" who sweep in and out of our lives, let's remember that the tool of choice Jesus wants to use is the sold-out individual who shows up, day after day, as a faithful and obedient follower of Christ.

As much as we have identified the strategic advantage for the church in our day, the church continues to face seemingly insurmountable challenges. These challenges are of such a magnitude, this will cause believers to reconsider where they truly stand in terms of a radical commitment to Christ and a seeking and trust in the power of the Holy Spirit to empower the believer to declare the uncompromised message of the love of God.

I once attended a banquet where Philip Yancey was the keynote speaker. He gave a very interesting talk on the dangers of a sleeping church in our society, by addressing the history of Christianity and showing where countries that once were key Christian centers are now, in regard to acknowledging or not acknowledging Christ as Savior. He challenged the audience to fast forward time by one hundred years and imagine where our society would be, in terms of a living Christian faith. He suggested a few negative scenarios that sounded perilously immediate, such as total oppression of prayer in schools, illegal expression of religion in public, and no Christian broadcasting of any kind in the media.

He then moved out from the podium and told the audience that he is convinced that God "moves". But he went on to say, in this case he didn't mean "move" in an exciting, supernatural, revivalist way; he meant that God, over history and in the present, literally moves by packing His boxes and suitcases and leaving.

To where does He move? To the places and to the people who have time for Him and who have not forgotten to include

Him in their daily affairs of life. The history of this planet clearly shows where Christianity was once the influential belief system, but is no longer. There are many examples, some of them closer than we might imagine — places such as Armenia, Turkey, and even Western Europe.

Western society now stands at a crucial point, facing a serious threat that God may pack up and move. The church is becoming more and more nominal and irrelevant in addressing the issues of our world; legislators are working hard to marginalize biblical truth and expression; and other faiths and religions are diluting the Christian presence.

So where do we go from here? The first place is to recognize that the opportunity is at our disposal to be fully engaged in the most rewarding and exciting activity in eternity — sharing our faith. Jesus called the disciples to look unto the fields and see that the harvest is ripe and ready for reaping. With the fracturing of our world today, in ways we would not have imagined just a few years ago, there is an openness for Christians to take their rightful position in the marketplaces of the world, to be the salt and light. With the dismantling of the artificial separation of "clergy" and "laity," and the recognition that each and every individual carries this treasure of the Good News in earthen vessels, we can involve ourselves in any one of thousands of unique ways to which God has called us.

Where we stand in history in respect to the mobility of our society, the availability of finances, and the great missionary wave of short term missions, there seems to be less of an excuse to not be a global missionary than ever before ... if there ever was such an excuse!

Hosea, the Old Testament prophet, sounded an alarm for the people of God. He called them to come back to God through repentance. In chapter six of his book we see that God had withdrawn His presence because of the ways they chose to live and the ungodly decisions they were making. He would stay away until several things happened in the minds and hearts of His people. One was that a confession would take place in the believers where there would be a verbal acknowledgement that they had sinned against God and were living in disobedience. God was waiting to see this occur before there was any engagement in a restored relationship with His people.

Any offense or sin committed in the Bible ultimately was not about the act itself, nor the hurt to others or to oneself, but was most importantly an act against God.

God was also seeking
to see repentance for sin — a determination and desire
to change thinking processes, habits, attitudes, lifestyles,
and opinions about Him.

Contrition is the second aspect of returning to God that God was looking for. Hosea was asking the people of God to recognize that the act of sin hurt God, and in turn damaged others and ourselves. Contrition is a more profound sense of grief than a verbal assent of a wrong done. It goes to the innermost person.

However, contrition can also be an emotional trigger that can provide temporary relief and satisfaction, but in the end does not create meaningful change. This is where many believers and leaders fall short when it comes to an earnest experience with God. Confession provides the tangible evidence that a wrong has been committed, but does not call for a change. The danger with a confession with no follow-through is that it can become the "right" thing to do to satisfy leadership or authorities, but can tend to be disingenuous.

Contrition is also something that is good and necessary; however, to stop here, we can satisfy ourselves and others that the emotional experience validates that we are right with God. But God calls for one more, crucial step.

The third event God was waiting for in their lives was repentance. Repentance, in the Bible, literally means a change of mind and direction; turning around and going the other way. God was waiting, not only to hear a confession or admission of wrong (which might be only lip service); nor a strong sense of contrition (which is a recognizing in a deep way the offensiveness of sin). God was also seeking to see repentance for sin — a determination and desire to change thinking processes, habits, attitudes, lifestyles, and opinions about Him.

---

*...needed is
faithful, available, and teachable believers
who are willing to take the time to come close
to God, to confess, to be contrite, and to repent and
throw yourself into the work God has for you.*

The present-day opportunities for cross-cultural communications through short-term missions call upon us to reawaken ourselves to the call of the Great Commission. They call us to recognize the window of opportunity that exists to engage in reaching others with the Gospel. They call us to respond to the challenges we face in our world. These three necessary activities must be accompanied by a true repentance before God, where confession is made, contrition is felt, and repentance occurs.

The next steps for you, as a reader of this book, are to consider your personal preparedness to follow in the footsteps of Christ, in living a life for others. Jesus called us to deny ourselves, take up our cross, and follow Him. Today, with the term Christianity being thrown around so loosely — to the point it no longer has a biblical meaning — we must re-consider what it means to be a follower of Christ. In light of eternity, the individual believer must ask the hard questions as to their goals and the alignment of those goals with the purposes of the Kingdom of God. They must ask hard questions about the time they have and whether it is time well spent, and if the price has been paid.

Many of us want the crown but are not willing to carry the cross. We desire the glory but are unwilling to enter into the grind of service to Christ in missions.

For the short term missionary, the call is to consider the next steps God would take you into in living a life for Him. Today, there are thousands of believers engaged in creative ways in mission work all over the world. Whether it is in a profession as a "tent maker," in traditional missionary work, or in support of mission organizations and local churches, the harvest is plentiful, the conditions are right, the threat is clear and present, the power of the Holy Spirit is available. All that is needed is faithful, available, and teachable believers who are willing to take the time to come close to God, to confess, to be contrite, and to repent and throw yourself into the work God has for you.

As we have seen throughout this book, God's passion for the lost is unfathomable. His method for restoring the broken relationship between Himself and His creation is the unconditional love of Christ, demonstrated on the cross. His tool to spread the news is the church, the people of God, walking in obedience and responding to the call of God to enter into and fulfill the Great Commission.

It is time to join the ranks and become part of the greatest force on earth; to see the greatest change in other lives, ever. With the creativity that God has dispensed there is no limit to what you can do in His service. This generation has the talent, the knowledge, and the extreme approach to life. But there has yet to be a full realization of the potential in the people of God of this generation ... perhaps the last generation before the return of Christ.

Summary:

Christianity is entirely inclusive, in that "God so loved the world." It is exclusive because Jesus is the only "way, the truth, the life." Everyone is invited into the Kingdom, but there is only one "Door."

Pillars of support for the cross-cultural communicator:

• The Church lives in a "post modern advantage," the realization that the anti-supernatural doctrine of the Enlightenment has been dissolved.

• The availability of information at a speed and volume never thought possible.

• High ideas are influencing the status quo.

• Jesus is actually an option today.

• The fact that in this postmodern society, all religions are considered equal, creates a positive edge for the believer.

• Human beings are implicitly believers. Today, society openly accepts that belief is a valid, deeply seated, closely-held concept.

Christianity is about relationship, unconditional love, forgiveness, community, grace, and acceptance. We are called to re-awaken ourselves to the call of the Great Commission, to recognize the window of opportunity that exists to engage in reaching others with the Gospel, to respond to the challenges we face in our world.

God's passion for the lost is unfathomable. His method for restoring the broken relationship between Himself and His creation is the unconditional love of Christ, demonstrated on the cross. His tool to spread the news is the church, the people of God, walking in obedience and responding to the call of God to enter into and fulfill the Great Commission.

CHAPTER EIGHT

Humility or Achievement?

Introduction

Should Christian leaders be humble, or should we go for the gold? This is one of the more challenging tensions found in spiritual leadership contexts today. I refer to the basic tension between the desire to move away from the paradigm of authoritarian leadership that can lead to abusive or controlling approaches and the need to see results and deliverables as responsible leaders. This tension — between humility and achievement — is healthy. Some may see the two as mutually exclusive, but I believe these are actually complementary concepts and characteristics that can live in harmony in a leader's life and world.

The gospel-writer Mark showed us the central theme his narrative in Jesus' statement: "For the Son of Man did not come into the world to be served but to serve and give His life a ransom for many" (10:45). This is the classic "humility and achievement" verse. Jesus is shown, coming as servant ("He humbled Himself") but also having a clear focus on outcome — His death on the cross for the sins of the world.

> Jesus operated with a bigger "yes"
> which empowered Him to be able to say "no"
> to the temptations, distractions,
> and allurements of natural enticements.

Throughout the gospels, we see the Satan vs. Jesus motif in events such as the killing of the babies by King Herod, the temptation of Jesus in the wilderness, the pressure and pursuit of the crowd to make Jesus an earthly king, the dying of His best friend Lazarus, the pleading of Peter for Jesus not to lay down His life, the prayer to let the cup of death to pass Him. These incidents, as well as many others, clearly reveal that in His humanity Jesus could have opted out of the eternal plan and settled for an alternative. However, Jesus operated with a bigger "yes" which empowered Him to be able to say "no" to the temptations, distractions, and allurements of natural enticements.

Jesus told his mother, Mary, that He must be about His Father's business; the gospel-writer Luke refers to Jesus setting His face toward Jerusalem like a flint, dramatically portraying the resolve He invoked to face His greatest hour.

Insights such as these reveal something different from the common understanding and values embraced by many leaders, who somehow find they are floundering in a quagmire of uncertainty, doubt, and fear in their efforts at decision-making. This is not the kind of humility Jesus showed.

The apostle Paul's definition of spirituality is quite different from what we may be used to in our spheres of spiritual leadership. When we meet Paul (first named Saul) in the book of Acts, there is little doubt that this is a proud, arrogant man. However, when we read his letters to the churches, we discover that Paul has sought to allow the Holy Spirit to free him from personal pride.

Paul refers to his ministry being marked by the constant application of service to people, and by a transparent honesty that his spiritual journey is not complete; in this life, he has not yet fully attained the level of spiritual growth to which he aspired.

He tells the church in Corinth that he is the least of all the apostles; however, he adds that he worked "harder than them all". Later, writing to the Ephesian church, he seems to have had an epiphany of humility, as he confesses that he is least of all the saints. In his letter to Timothy his understudy and successor in ministry, he declares that he is the worst of all "sinners".

As we read these statements, we must wonder, did Paul somehow lose his way and drift from his lofty spiritual heights as his life and ministry moved on — or is there something far more valuable here for us to learn?

Paul's letters to Timothy are understood to be some of his last writings before Paul became a martyr for Jesus. As Paul faces the possibility that his mission on earth was near the end, he claims that he has fought the good fight; he is confident that there is laid up for him a crown of eternal life. He writes with the vision and vigor he always expresses. So there must be something else here that speaks to us concerning the pursuit of humility and desire for achievement.

> All of this translates into a spiritual dance which develops trust, growth, maturity, desire, and greater intimacy.

Let me suggest that, as Paul grew in the revelation of who God is, the recognition of God's wholly otherness was so apparent and fantastic that in comparison Paul's holiness — and ours — became insignificant. The greater the revelation of God, the greater the awareness of our inadequacy before Him, and the greater the realization of His supremacy and brilliance leading to our dependence upon Him.

Paul knew he had fought the good fight; he also knew better than to take credit for his success — that credit all goes to God. Paul understood the balance between humility and achievement.

We, as flawed human beings, seek prescriptive solutions in leadership which are nothing more than short cuts or pat answers; but God provides to His people leaders in process, leaders who balance achievement with humility, and balance humility with a desire to accomplish much for the Kingdom. All of this translates into a spiritual dance which develops trust, growth, maturity, desire, and greater intimacy.

Our lives and our leadership is like the commercial from a technology company that depicts a plane in full flight while a crew is building it "on the fly." The commercial suggests, "that is what we do." Leaders are not called to have it all together personally before they launch out or to become impervious to the problems, challenges, and distractions of other "mere mortals". Nor are they called to perfect situations. Much like building the airplane on the fly, they are in process themselves, and inherit imperfect circumstances to work on. Leaders are called to literally lead on the fly, to build while in the air.

Leadership Accelerators

My sons, Jordan and Christopher, and I had an opportunity to be trained as qualified scuba divers by my brother, who is a master diver. The process included reading a book, taking a written test, some class instruction, and finally the practical lessons in the water. We soon learned that your first dive is not into the great abyss — it's not, away you go merrily on your own to enjoy the great sport of diving and discover unknown worlds.

Learning to dive involves a series of "tentative" dives to go over and over the basics in equipment and safety lessons. After about three outings in the water, the time finally comes to descend to the sixty-foot depth. At that point it is easy to realize why it is so important to have as much repetition as possible in shallow water, before going deeper. The fantastic experience of being under water and the fascination become so distracting that it would be easy to forget even the simplest of functions or safety maneuvers. It's difficult to remember to just check your watch to see the time spent under water, the initial times you're in the water. After all who has time to look at your watch when there is so much to see and do under water!

At the sixty-foot depth, one of the lessons involves learning to depend upon your "buddy" when performing an emergency ascent. That's in case something critical happens where you must ascend to the surface of the water — you communicate to your buddy and share air as you go up. One by one, we were to perform this procedure. Several had gone up before the next person to try was my oldest son Jordan. However, he ended up panicking, and was seriously motivated to ascend as quickly as possible, which can be very dangerous. What I saw from my place under water was someone who was throwing off his mask, weight belt and regulator, who was pushing away his buddy, refusing to share air from the buddy's regulator, and doing anything else possible, all in an attempt to save himself. I later came to learn that what happened was called "equipment rejection." This occurs during a time of panic; it is counter intuitive, leading the person to do the opposite of actions that would save himself or herself in an emergency.

Leaders today can very easily fall into the counter intuitive trap of equipment rejection, and too often do. Its symptoms often can be detected in phrases such as, "God wants me to be used in my greatest area of weakness!" or "if we rely on our strengths we cannot exercise faith and dependence on God and so we shouldn't use them".

One flaw in this thinking is the assumption that people who use their gifts don't depend on God or need faith to accomplish what He has asked them to do. Another flaw in this type of thinking is the unspoken presumption that God gives us gifts, abilities, and skills, but somehow directs us to not utilize them!

This thinking can arise because of insecurity in themselves, or a lack of understanding of the tools available for use in the art of leading, or from a mindset of "sacred and spiritual" that often clouds the issue.

Insecurity is one of the killers of spiritual leadership. This is evidenced when a leader lacks inner confidence, and perceives transparency as an enemy to be fought rather than embraced.

As leaders, we often thwart the advancement of the Kingdom of God due to unexplored concepts, personal convictions laid over the body as absolutes, or underdeveloped thinking. Why would God grace us and gift us with heavenly things and then deprive us from using and enjoying them? More importantly, what kind of God would He be if He were to act in this way? What kind of individuals are we?

I have come to the conclusion that the "mystical" conclusions we come up with are simply excuses for us not to exercise the gifts and abilities God has given us. They reflect a pseudo humility that stunts our growth, and a lack of faith in God — we act as though using the gifts might threaten God, that He cannot take care of us should we abuse the gifts and abilities or use them for something other than His glory. That would be a weak God, indeed.

> Leaders today can very easily fall into the counter intuitive trap of equipment rejection, and too often do.

It is time for God's people to rise up and change things now, instead of fiddling around with laying down our gifts and abilities to "learn" new ones in order to be humble and have faith. What happens next if we are to take this approach? Once we learn something new, do we lay it down again so that we can be used in another area of weakness?

This trend will lead us straight down a path of being useless vessels for God.

The other danger is that of reinforcing our insecurity because we never take full advantage of our place in the Kingdom, and therefore feel all the more insecure for an indefinite period of time. The Bible calls on us to not think more highly of ourselves than we should, but to have a sober judgment. Today we have exchanged this healthy assessment for something that is twisted and a device of the enemy. I strongly believe that this mindset has allowed us, as leaders, to default to spiritualizing away the need for the hard work needed to learn and apply effective skills to exercise our leadership responsibility.

When a spiritual leader moves out on his or her own, things can go south in a hurry. I remember one particular dark season in my life when it seemed that there was a full frontal attack on my life. Finances, family, ministry, friends, and more, all seemed to be in a state of chaos.

> When God puts His leader on the potter's wheel, it hurts, it is frustrating, and all kinds of things are revealed about ourselves — impatience, anger, self-pity, revenge, jealousy, etc. — and that is exactly why God puts us on the wheel in the first place.

I was losing control on all fronts, and my reaction was to try and grasp at any semblance of control. When I fell into faulty thinking of this kind, it only made things worse; I began to repel people, rather than create stability for myself. A very good friend of mine, who is a clinical psychologist, was brave enough to call me on my attitude, saying that if I didn't deal with the hostility in my life, I would become an island. I would end up shutting out even the best of friends. With the grace of God, family and friends, I was able to deal the issues and see, over time, some truly miraculous events take place in my life. It is amazing how fast a person can rebound from an emotional, spiritual, and psychological challenge. We all too often think it will take months or years, and that, in the meantime, we are no good to God or others. This is simply not true. God can carry us through all these situations on a time line that is fantastically rapid.

I call these times in the life of a leader, "spiritual accelerators." These are things brought out in our lives that put us on the potter's wheel for adjustments, repairs, and renovations in God. Immediately after a particular period of time in ministry with the disciples, Jesus decided to stay and pray while He sent the disciples to the other side of the lake in a boat. As they rowed away, a storm brewed up and they feared for their lives. In the midst of this event, Jesus appears and a wonderful revelation of Him occurs before He gets into the boat.

The conclusion of this story is that "suddenly," they found themselves at their destination on the other shore. If we are open and alert, we can see the "suddenlies" or the spiritual accelerators in our lives, as God does His transforming work in us.

I recently was working with an individual who needed some counsel as well as emotional healing. My thinking on the matter was, once the main issue was identified, that was just the beginning and it would take years for the individual to get "up to speed." However, as we walked through the issues, it was amazing how fast the recuperation and healing came about.

When God puts His leader on the potter's wheel, it hurts, it is frustrating, and all kinds of things are revealed about ourselves — impatience, anger, self-pity, revenge, jealousy, etc. — and that is exactly why God puts us on the wheel in the first place. In the times of heat, being re-formed, placed on the shelf, and broken once again, deeply seated frailties are exposed. His intention is to conform us into the image of Christ. As followers of Christ, this is of course our stated prayer as well — but when God answers us, it rarely looks like what we asked or expected. As a matter of fact, we discover that God took our pleas more seriously than we did ourselves.

Effective leadership will take on the spiritual accelerators in our lives and allow God to work them out for our benefit. If we — or others — were to attempt to artificially create these events, we would break for good under the tremendous exposure. However, God knows us intimately. He caringly and tenderly shepherds us through the stages of growth until we attain full maturity in Christ. Both the practical and spiritual accelerators are tools to help us to achieve ultimate outcomes.

> ...if vision is the wind that propels a leader toward the future, implementation is the rudder that guides the leader and his or her team toward making that vision reality.

Relating and relaxing, not racing

Nothing in this discussion is about doing — we are focused on being. I had the privilege recently to be at a conference where Stuart McAlpine was teaching. He challenged those who were there with the need to visit Bethany and hang out with Jesus. For Jesus, Bethany was a place of respite.

I had a phone call recently from Randy Sonchen, the World Missions Director for the Pentecostal Assemblies of Canada. After discussing setting up the objectives for a national short term missions project, Randy said to me, "the relational aspect of what we are doing is the tangible!" I could not agree more.

It seems to me that many leaders in the Kingdom of God do not understand the power of being with Jesus in Bethany. That is where our relationship with Him can be strengthened. And our relationship with Christ is the source — from here, things begin to happen that we could never have imagined in the first place.

It is in times of retreat and withdrawal that the leader

gets centered and focused — not in the heat of the battle or the entering into the temptation of becoming the proverbial activist. The leader will discover that there are three primary areas of focus which need attention; these areas are all discovered and developed in the relating and relaxing zone.

The first is the vision he or she carries; the second is the competency to implement the vision; the third, to keep in mind and act upon the succession principle.

"Vision," for the leader, is the oxygen that propels him or her forward. The metaphor is not accidental — for a leader, vision is as necessary as oxygen. The tools for this aspect of leadership include having a vast, compelling picture of how things can be; and being able in a concise and clear way to communicate that vision to others, so they can catch the passion and join in attempting to realize it.

"Implementation" is the practical part, where the leader has a sufficiently high level of competence to roll out the vision and create steps to see the vision happen. This is where leaders far too often fail. To change metaphors slightly, if vision is the wind that propels a leader toward the future, implementation is the rudder that guides the leader and his or her team toward making that vision reality.

Leaders fall into several categories when it comes the implementation stage. There is the mystic, who believes that once a vision is received, then God does the rest.

There is the abdicator, who is secure enough to admit that he does not have all the skills to implement the vision, but who then completely passes it off to another, utterly losing control.

There is the paranoid, who insists on owning completely the implementation stage, although he has insufficient competence and ends up in frustration, abandoning the vision and moving onto the next "flavor of the month."

And there is the leader who realizes that a mature and responsible leader develops whatever competencies they require to ensure the ownership and realization of the vision. That being said, it is important to understand competencies are not developed to keep others from assisting; we're not arguing against delegation and team-work. Instead, competencies for leaders mean developing the critical skills in the areas of selecting a team, empowering others, and leading others in the vision.

A competent leader will always seek to become inclusive of others, welcoming others who come along with better skills in varying areas to help to see the vision fulfilled.

The third stage, "succession," is often neglected or misunderstood. In short, succession is a responsibility which must be exercised by leaders in order to ensure sustainability and capacity of the vision. Succession calls for the leader to have a mindset that God has called them to be involved in something that must include others, and which eventually must be led by others. Whether they are actually engaged in the work themselves, oversee the work, or are called upon to keep the work on their radar screen for accountability, leaders have taken upon themselves an unreasonable amount of burden. While accomplishing the vision can be very invigorating, a leader who sees no end to the burden may find their enthusiasm turning sour. Burn-out, disappointment, and resignation can await the leader who operates in this toxic environment.

The succession aspect allows a leader to continually look for and be aware of other leaders and potential leaders who can be included and groomed for the vision. Our role is to obey the call to vision, develop others to participate in that vision, and to pass off any aspect of the vision to others to carry and share the load. This may include any part of the work to be done, or all of it, so that the leader can continue to focus on his or her primary call or even move on to something else.

This kind of leadership activity cannot be engaged in "on

the fly," racing toward nowhere fast. This is where understanding the paradox of humility and achievement remains important. A leader must be pleased about achieving the vision, but be humble enough to look for succession opportunities. If leaders do not walk in this path, we are doomed to repeat the mistakes of the past over and over again.

> Succession calls for the leader to have a mindset that God has called them to be involved in something that must include others, and which eventually must be led by others.

We do not have to go far to see this played out in the life of Jesus as we follow His ministry in the Gospels. He preaches and attracts followers. He teaches the followers and sends them out. He leaves them and they continue the work. Then the leaders follow His model and pass on the same modus operandi to their disciples. There was a constant off-loading of leadership activities and responsibilities to faithful people.

And there is always enough leadership responsibility to go around. It reminds me of the two approaches demographers use in studying our world. Some refer to a sum total economic reality, where there is only so much food supply over against the population, or only so much opportunity for people in a stagnant market. Others argue that there is unlimited potential for expanding food supplies and economic opportunities.

I believe that the reality is, life does not constitute only "so many pieces of the pie" but — economically or otherwise — it is always expanding and there is enough in life, and more that enough!

Leaders sometimes fear that when taken literally, passing on vision and implementing a succession plan, will leave a vacuum for the leader; after the responsibility is passed on, the leader will have nothing to do, and may even be seen as being delinquent in the exercising of their duties. Believe me, nothing could be further from the truth — there is enough, and more than enough to do in growing the Kingdom of God.

A friend of mine is a pastor in a growing local church. He shared with me how his training in a fast food franchise formed his leadership style. As he set out to become management material, his attitude and approach was to work hard, fill in anywhere possible, be seen busy at anything that might require attention. But when the upper management came by to evaluate his progress, he discovered to his dismay that they were not pleased with him at all. They told him that if he wanted to move into greater areas of responsibility, he would have to significantly adjust his approach to work.

A leader needs to begin the day deciding what he or she is going to do, because if not, someone else will plan it — and a leader needs to believe that he or she can plan it better than someone else can.

What they were concerned about was his activist manner that made him look busy but moved him off the objective to lead. What the management wanted to see was an up and coming leader, ensuring that the work was getting done by those assigned and responsible for that aspect of work. They informed him that, when they walk in to assess him in the future, they wanted to see a potential leader who is overseeing and observing and directing — not manually working.

Applied to my friend's current context of pastoral ministry, it is amazing to see how that "simple" understanding has led to him having a healthy integrated life, empowered and motivated leaders in the church, and a life cadence that is easy but making strong reverberations throughout the city he is ministering in. Essentially, he is becoming and has become a leader who understands the balance between humility and achievement. By choosing others in whom to invest, developing them, directing them and empowering them, he is exercising humility in his work. He is not the one to do all the work nor the hero of the local church.

At the same time, by applying these leadership principles he is accelerating toward achieving his calling and resolve — to see a healthy local church and a community impacted by outreach. It is a gross overreaction — in fact, it is a false assumption — that when a leader is exercising succession, they are not executing leadership or they are walking away from responsibility. In reality, they are assessing their mission-critical activities, exercising conscious living, and intentionally choosing to focus on their priorities.

These are the leaders who wake up each day and ask themselves, "What business am I in, and how's business?" They're making the hard decisions to align themselves to that priority. A leader needs to begin the day deciding what he or she is going to do, because if not, someone else will plan it — and a leader needs to believe that he or she can plan it better than someone else can.

Leadership qualities

The importance of succession and teamwork in general means that, if you are a leader, you must always be looking for other leaders. What qualities should you look for in healthy leaders?

These qualities are really not obscure; they're not hidden treasures to be painstakingly pried open. But giving some attention to the issue will make it easier for you to identify, in confidence, the qualities of a leader. This should also, by the way, help you to be a better leader yourself.

The leader knows the difference between activity and meaningful work. An active, full day or agenda is sometimes seen as synonymous with hard-working, busy leaders who are on the rise. Studies actually reveal that this may not be the case. This busy-ness may point to the "unintentional leader" who lives for the feedback of others and occupies himself or herself with activity that is counterproductive to the responsibility called for. Just because the day is filled with things to do does not signify work is accomplished in leadership.

> If we are going to become effective and successful leaders, we must live our leadership out in this area. I believe we need to reframe our understanding of what accountability is.

Meaningful work is work related to the mission, vision, and values of the organization or the personal sense of calling one has. Meaningful work will also reflect a strong sense of inner direction that is healthy and centered, operating on principle rather than for the emotional stroking gained by activity. Self-consciousness, ability to perform the related work, and a compelling purpose are the three elements of the leader engrossed in meaningful work instead of activity.

Another significant quality of healthy leadership is that the leader functions at the cusp of his or her leadership abilities. Professionals in all arenas of life have an ability to push themselves and their particular tools to the place where "in control" and "out of control" are almost indistinguishable. This is the "zone," the place of optimum return and success.

As leaders, it is easy to operate within comfort zones, way within the limit of toleration, while we act as though we are on the edge. That's fraud, not leadership. As in the case of the sports professional, spiritual leadership calls for us to continue to lead by being out in front, maximizing our leadership gifts and roles to inspire and provide an example for others we are influencing.

Leaders are also to ensure that they are taking responsibility for the consequences of their actions and that they are exercising accountability. We seem to hear these words often, but sadly, they seem to be used more in rhetoric and not in practice. Leaders will live in responsibility and accountability.

Warren Weirsbe once said that accountability is the gift you give yourself. Too often, though, accountability seems to be something that a leader urges others to practice, but fails to practice himself.

If we are going to become effective and successful leaders, we must live our leadership out in this area. I believe we need to reframe our understanding of what accountability is.

While the abuse of accountability has become the things of legend — just read the business pages, almost any day; or, sadly, the churches pages, too many days — this does not mean we can give up on being accountable. Accountability continues to have a central place in biblical leadership; but we need to understand that accountability is not something someone does to you, but something you incorporate into yourself to ensure that you adhere to the values you embrace.

Are you accountable to others? Yes. But first, you must be accountable to yourself, before God. That is the key. Most leaders I have met sincerely and earnestly desire to have a strong moral and ethical walk. Most want to see change in themselves in order to perform at peak. These desires, coupled with a strong accountability strategy, can go a long way to realizing these noble goals.

The other term in this quality statement is the word responsible. I like how Stephen R. Covey in his outstanding book, The Seven Habits of Highly Effective People, points out that the two words that make up this word are "response" and "ability." In other words, as human beings we have the ability to exercise what the animal kingdom cannot, that of taking the time to respond to situations in place of reacting to them out of instinct. God gave us two ends to use, one to sit on and the other to think — heads we win and tails we lose!

Responsibility is exercising leadership with a clear mind and heart, assessing the lay of the land, and in place of reacting out of being overwhelmed or overconfident, it is responding to a preconceived plan with the foresight that God has blessed us with.

Leadership also calls us to not back away from risk, and to stand up for principles God has embedded into us. Each and every decision a leader makes is a risk. Andy Grove, former C.E.O of Intel, once said in an interview that leadership is sitting on the lead horse of a large team and proclaiming that everyone needs to leave the mountain they are presently on, and charging down it into the valley and up the next mountain. This, all the while not being sure that particular mountain is really the right one, nor being able to see what is in the foggy valley below any more than those who are following, yet leading the charge anyway.

Leaders, by definition, make decisions. They may make good ones or bad ones, but decisions they must make. A key quality of a leader is the ability to perceive the bigger picture in the organization, and the intentional application of that insight to make vision become reality. Leaders do this by exercising extreme focus on the ultimate objective, and ensuring that everything done by them and their team ties into that ultimate objective.

Assessment, evaluation, reflection, and dialog are all aspects that keep the mission in alignment and going in the right direction. Leaders strive for excellence in all that they do, which simply means that they have a recognition there is ground to be taken, and that while perfection is an elusive concept, continuous improvement is the staple diet of the successful leaders. Wherever an area of improvement is possible, the leader ensures that he or she, or others in the organization, are on top of it, ensuring that a system is developed so others can follow and apply the critical success factors as well.

> …a leader who is creating opportunities for relationships to be established, where others are sought out for advice and input, and where a sense of family is nurtured.

The leader also is constantly seeking out opportunities to inspire others to do their best, to become strong stakeholders in the objectives and mission of the organization, and to rise to the call. The team will understand that this is not the thoughtless type of leader who barks out commands and operates on a shame/guilt paradigm, but this is a leader who is creating opportunities for relationships to be established, where others are sought out for advice and input, and where a sense of family is nurtured.

The tell-tail marks of leadership are; the exercise of courage, the incorporation of passion, the application of humility, the acceptance and expression of humanity, and a quickening spirit.

Conclusion

Today, spiritual leadership calls for a true combination of humility and achievement, especially because of the world in which we find ourselves. As you have read in previous chapters, the post modern society we live in can have its advantages — people are more open and accepting of spirituality than in recent decades — but it has also created "liquidity" in

Christianity where experiential expression does not necessarily require absolutes or a moral imperative.

As a result, the leader is discovering more and more that leadership is exercised without a plumb line to call the church back to. Leaders cannot appeal to corporate branding (this is the way you must follow!) or to obedience to commands. Nor can it default to a passive acceptance of, let alone embrace, the "new spirituality" that has abused the term grace until it is no longer recognizable.

Today, leaders must approach issues and people in true humility, confronting the arrogance of the thinking of today's spirituality with an humble spirit, immense courage and fierce resolve to stand strong.

> The tell-tail marks of leadership are;
> the exercise of courage, the incorporation
> of passion, the application of humility,
> the acceptance and expression of humanity,
> and a quickening spirit.
> Today, spiritual leadership calls for
> a true combination of humility and achievement.

I wrote earlier in the book of an event at which Philip Yancey spoke. He pointed to the historical trend in the church where it has seen countries and peoples once impacted by God's Spirit now devoid of anything resembling Christianity. His conclusion was that God moves, but not in the way we traditionally understand that term. Yancey said that God in essence packs His bags and moves to where people have time for Him.

For me, this is an accurate portrait of where we are at

today. Our responsibility as leaders is to call the church and society back to taking time out with God. To once again enter into the romance to which He has called us. To nurture an intimate relationship whereby He can heal us of our diseases, fill us once again, turn our hearts to His person and priorities.

This will take leadership that is focused, competent, determined and models the way. It will take leadership that rejects definitions of leadership imposed by society. It will take leadership that once again begins to believe what God says about the church and behaves accordingly.

Leadership will have to slay the idol of "ministry," where it is easy to hide and to create a pretense of spirituality and effective leadership. Instead, leaders must create a strategy of leadership that reflects Kingdom priorities of prayer, community, and practice.

Leadership will have to repent of the intimidation it has succumbed to and break away from the "group think" it has been involved with — nodding our heads and affirming others because of insecurity and the fear of man.

Leadership will need to stop pretending that it has jumped a great chasm while it remains on the same side as those they wish to lead. Leaders must exercise great courage and skill in actually taking the leap to which we know we are called.

Agreement is not enough. Verbally assenting to the new paradigms God is calling us to be is not the same as implementing them into our lives and bringing others graciously and patiently into them as well.

Leadership is not entering into a competition with fellow leaders but is instead reaching out to exceed one's personal best. It is focusing on where we should be, in place of exposing where others are not, only to make our own fruitless lives feel better.

Organizations and followers are indicative of the life of

their leaders. Based upon this reality, what does our leadership look like? Why is it so difficult to move away from the things that are destroying the good work of God and toward the things that will lead us further down the road?

> ...as leaders, we have let our knowledge about leadership get ahead of our reality and ended up over-promising and under-delivering.

One reason is ignorance of the role we play as leaders, and of the need to exercise healthy leadership. Another is the fact that in order to justify our existence, events have overshadowed the process, leading to the "flavor of the month" and the "quick fix" syndromes. Yet another is the classic frog in the kettle syndrome, whereby we have slowly adjusted to the temperature of our times instead of acting upon it with truth and grace. And another is that, as leaders, we have let our knowledge about leadership get ahead of our reality and ended up over-promising and under-delivering.

The call goes forth for more Nehemiahs who fear neither the "secular" tools we have at our disposal to use for the Kingdom of God, nor the "spiritual" tools provided us. For leaders who, like Nehemiah, are compelled by an outrageous reality, moved to the deepest seat of the emotions, launch a very real and practical strategy to resolve the situation, model the way it should be done, gain a following from true integrity and leadership, and walk in the favor of God.

CONCLUSION

Why Short Term Missions?

Short term missions has been around for decades, in the form in which it now exists. The primary focus of short term missions is to fulfill the Great Commission through the mobilizing of individuals and teams via the local church.

"Short term missions" is defined as an individual or team involving themselves in a cross-cultural missions experience for a length of time up to two years less a day. In order to achieve the task at hand, more needs to be done in the area of creating awareness and opportunities that will facilitate missions. Short term missions has seen such widespread growth that there are an estimated one million people in North America going overseas on short term mission trips each year. Add to this the fact that other countries in the western world and in developing regions, are experiencing the same dynamic, and the picture is clear — God is blessing in this area.

> Short term missions serves as the vehicle to fulfill the response of the thousands of people who have taken seriously the thousands of public challenges to "Go into all the world and make disciples".

Short term missions is best utilized alongside existing mission organizations, internationally and in the area of opening up new opportunities in restricted-access countries. It involves a shift, from the local church being simply a promotional agency or financial funding tool for missions, to the local church being the mission-sending agency where people can be challenged, trained, and sent out to the mission field. In this way there is a recognition of the amazing potential for all believers to be used by God to accomplish the Great Commission.

In turn, short term mission teams come back to the local church where they are well received and where they become key workers in the areas of marketplace evangelism, local church ministry, and in general, leaders for the Kingdom of God.

Based upon the strong teaching in the Bible that God gave gifts to every person who believes in Him, and that God has a calling upon everyone's life, short term missions intentionally mines the gifts and calling of people and releases them for intentional purposes in reaching the unchurched. Short term missions serves as the vehicle to fulfill the response of the thousands of people who have taken seriously the thousands of public challenges to "Go into all the world and make disciples". It also seizes upon the context of our times, where extreme living, high mobility, effective educational delivery systems, and available funding are at an unprecedented point in our culture.

Short term missions, at the beginning of the 21st century, is a responsive ministry creating the opportunity the church has prayed for over the past several decades ... that laborers would be sent into the harvest field. It also is the seedbed of a host of people who will be impacted by the direct experience of the mission field, and who will consider their future in light of the call of God and global need.

Short term missions is also the delivery system that is needed in order to break up the blockages that have existed due to a highly centralized governance system. In essence, this means anyone can participate in the affairs of the Kingdom, where once only the servicing of the few was possible, due to heavy structural restrictions.

Around the world, local churches are becoming sending churches, creating a tidal wave of activity that is ushering countless of individuals into the Kingdom of God. It is literally creating a revolution, dispelling disillusionment of church adherents and building momentum and confidence that the task can be accomplished. If it were any other way, why would God have called us to the Great Commission?

The challenge to local church leadership is to maintain a high level of focus and vigilance to the mandate of world missions. For leadership to accomplish this, they must create a crystal clear message, which they must follow, themselves, and which they must convey to the Body of Christ at large.

Leadership will also need to appreciate the new role laid

before them, to operate in a more collegial context rather than a self contained one. To rely on other leaders' gifts and expertise calls upon a deep sense of security as well as openness to learn. This synergistic approach will grow leadership generally; it will allow for high levels of quality benchmarks in short term missions; it will result in the sum total being greater than the individual parts. The potential then becomes the reality, as leadership, local churches, mission organizations, and the mission field cooperate as never before.

> The shift here
> is from a competitive approach
> toward a more relational one focusing
> upon the task at hand.
> The focus shifts from building of one's
> own ministry to taking on the task at hand.

The shift here is from a competitive approach toward a more relational one focusing upon the task at hand. The focus shifts from building of one's own ministry to taking on the task at hand. Besides, when did the work of the Kingdom of God ever qualify as anyone's own, exclusive ministry?

In order for this shift to be accomplished, an understanding that ministry, missions, and the Kingdom of God are not a "zero sum" entity is imperative. Global missions and the mobilizing of thousands of short term missions teams is a massive undertaking and cannot be accomplished just through seeking our own niche ministries, but also through joining the ranks alongside all others who are focused on seeing the Great Commission fulfilled.

Summary:

The basic assumption must be that the mission field, indigenous worker, missionary, missions agency, denominations, mission organization, and local church are all the conduit God has chosen to use on this planet to express His love and grace. And any or all these various expressions are sincere, intentional, and obsessed with the Great Commission. All have a significant role to fulfill, despite the differing methodologies.

Effectiveness is realized when the "team" comes together and shares our perspectives, networks, experiences, and insights. It is the cumulative successes that count and which are to be celebrated. By all of us.

FOR MORE INFORMATION CONTACT:

Lee Primeau
7867 Springbank Way SW
Calgary, Alberta, Canada
T3H 4J7

missionshift@esolconnect.com

Phone: (403) 710-2169

"This book is about developing a framework for successful and effective communications in an uncertain world".

Communication and mission work is not easy. Varied dynamics and unpredictable context mean the experience calls on every resource one can summon. It exposes flaws like insecurity, defensiveness, emotional toxicity, panic, and withdrawal. However, in international or domestic environments, effective communication is essential for success. According to Lee Primeau, by developing proper cross-cultural communication skills, these challenges can be overcome.

In Mission_Shift, Lee brings a fresh, challenging approach to developing cross-cultural communication skills. Lee draws from twenty years of extensive international work and travel, and as a researcher and lecturer.

Mission_Shift explores the new landscape of missions and international ministry. Lee deals with the implications of post-modernity, biblical context, and the dynamics of cross-cultural communication for successful and effective ministry. He provides guidelines for becoming "international-able" for anyone contemplating working, traveling, or ministering in a cross-cultural context.

Lee Primeau

Lee Primeau is the Project Coordinator for the STM Network of the Pentecostal Assemblies of Canada. Lee is also the C.E.O. and co-founder of eSO'L Connection Inc., providing high security and virtual office collaboration to the international business community. He is in demand internationally as a lecturer, speaker, and consultant in both the NGO and private sectors. Lee lives with his wife, Cathy, and their sons, Jordan and Christopher, in western Canada.

$16.95 US / $19.95 CDN

Copyright © LEE PRIMEAU. All rights reserved. Printed in Canada.

Cover design

www.blessad.ca

www.ingramcontent.com/pod-product-compliance
Lightning Source LLC
Chambersburg PA
CBHW060526090426
42735CB00011B/2387